JOHN

God in the Flesh
John 1–10

Group Directory

**Pass this Directory around and have your Group Members
fill in their names and phone numbers**

Name	Phone
_____	_____
_____	_____
_____	_____
_____	_____
_____	_____
_____	_____
_____	_____
_____	_____
_____	_____
_____	_____
_____	_____
_____	_____
_____	_____
_____	_____

JOHN
God in the Flesh

PROJECT DIRECTOR:
James F. Couch, Jr.

WRITING & EDITORIAL TEAM:
Keith Madsen, Cathy Tardif, Katy Harris

PRODUCTION TEAM:
Sharon Penington, Erika Tiepel

SERENDIPITY HOUSE • NASHVILLE, TENNESSEE

John: God in the Flesh
© 2002 Serendipity House
Fifth Printing October 2007

Published by Serendipity House Publishers
Nashville, Tennessee

ISBN: 1-5749-4095-3
Item No. 001197642

Dewey Decimal Classification: 232.955
Subject Headings:
JESUS CHRIST–MIRACLES / BIBLE. N.T. GOSPELS–STUDY / CHRISTIAN LIFE

Unless otherwise indicated, all Scripture quotations are taken from the
Holman Christian Standard Bible®,
Copyright © 1999, 2000, 2002, 2003 by Holman Bible Publishers. Used by permission.

To purchase additional copies of this resource or other studies:
ORDER ONLINE at www.SerendipityHouse.com
WRITE Serendipity House, One LifeWay Plaza, Nashville, TN 37234
FAX (615) 277-8181
PHONE (800) 525-9563

1-800-525-9563
www.SerendipityHouse.com

Printed in the United States of America

TABLE OF CONTENTS

CORE VALUES

Community: The purpose of this curriculum is to build community within the body of believers around Jesus Christ.

Group Process: To build community, the curriculum must be designed to take a group through a step-by-step process of sharing your story with one another.

Interactive Bible Study: To share your "story," the approach to Scripture in the curriculum needs to be open-ended and right brain—to "level the playing field" and encourage everyone to share.

Developmental Stages: To provide a healthy program throughout the four stages of the life cycle of a group, the curriculum needs to offer courses on three levels of commitment: (1) Beginner Level—low-level entry, high structure, to level the playing field; (2) Growth Level—deeper Bible study, flexible structure, to encourage group accountability; (3) Discipleship Level—in-depth Bible study, open structure, to move the group into high gear.

Target Audiences: To build community throughout the culture of the church, the curriculum needs to be flexible, adaptable and transferable into the structure of the average church.

INTRODUCTION

Each healthy small group will move through various stages as it matures.

Growth Stage: Here the group begins to care for one another as it learns to apply what they learn through Bible study, worship and prayer.

Develop Stage: The inductive Bible study deepens while the group members discover and develop gifts and skills. The group explores ways to invite their neighbors and coworkers to group meetings.

Birth Stage: This is the time in which group members form relationships and begin to develop community. The group will spend more time in ice-breaker exercises, relational Bible study and covenant building.

Multiply Stage: The group begins the multiplication process. Members pray about their involvement in new groups. The "new" groups begin the lifecycle again with the Birth Stage.

 **Subgrouping:** If you have nine or more people at a meeting, Serendipity recommends you divide into subgroups of 3–6 for the Bible study. Ask one person to be the leader of each subgroup and to follow the directions for the Bible study. After 30 minutes, the Group Leader will call "time" and ask all subgroups to come together for the Caring Time.

Each group meeting should include all parts of the "three-part agenda."

Ice-Breaker: Fun, history-giving questions are designed to warm the group and to build understanding about the other group members. You can choose to use all of the Ice-Breaker questions, especially if there is a new group member that will need help in feeling comfortable with the group.

Bible Study: The heart of each meeting is the reading and examination of the Bible. The questions are open, discover questions that lead to further inquiry. Reference notes are provided to give everyone a "level playing field." The emphasis is on understanding what the Bible says and applying the truth to real life. The questions for each session build. There is always at least one "going deeper" question provided. You should always leave time for the last of the "questions for interaction." Should you choose, you can use the optional "going deeper" question to satisfy the desire for the challenging questions in groups that have been together for a while.

Caring Time: All study should point us to actions. Each session ends with prayer and direction in caring for the needs of the group members. You can choose between several questions. You should always pray for the "empty chair." Who do you know that could fill that void in your group?

Sharing Your Story: These sessions are designed for members to share a little of their personal lives each time. Through a number of special techniques each member is encouraged to move from low risk less personal sharing to higher risk responses. This helps develop the sense of community and facilitates care giving.

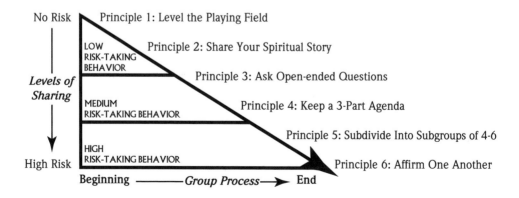

Group Covenant: A group covenant is a "contract" that spells out your expectations and the ground rules for your group. It's very important that your group discuss these issues—preferably as part of the first session.

GROUND RULES:

- *Priority:* While you are in the group, you give the group meeting priority.

- *Participation:* Everyone participates and no one dominates.

- *Respect:* Everyone is given the right to their own opinion and all questions are encouraged and respected.

- *Confidentiality:* Anything that is said in the meeting is never repeated outside the meeting.

- *Empty Chair:* The group stays open to new people at every meeting.

- *Support:* Permission is given to call upon each other in time of need—even in the middle of the night.

- *Advice Giving:* Unsolicited advice is not allowed.

- *Mission:* We agree to do everything in our power to start a new group as our mission.

ISSUES:

- The time and place this group is going to meet is:_____

- Responsibility for refreshments is: _____

- Childcare is _____ responsibility.

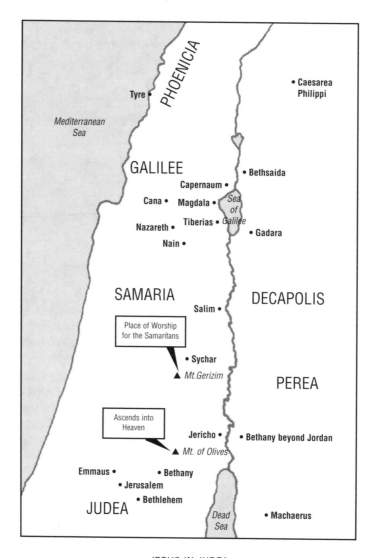

JESUS IN JUDEA

- **Sychar**—Talks with woman at well

- **Emmaus**—Appears to two after resurrection

- **Jericho**—Heals blind Bartimaeus; calls Zacchaeus down from tree

- **Jerusalem**—Clears the temple; crucifixion and resurrection

- **Bethany**—Raises Lazarus from the dead; anointed in Simon the Leper's house

- **Bethlehem**—Birth

- **Bethany beyond Jordan**—Traditional site of the baptism by John the Baptist

SESSION 1
THE WORD BECAME FLESH

SCRIPTURE   JOHN 1:1–18

INTRODUCTION TO THE BOOK OF JOHN

Welcome to this study of John! Together we will learn to appreciate our Savior anew as we discover what it means that Jesus came into the world as the Word made flesh.

The writer of the fourth Gospel does not name himself in the text. Like the other three Gospels, the fourth one is anonymous. Yet in a curious way the fourth one is less anonymous than the other three because the writer identifies himself by way of a title. When he refers to the disciple John, he calls him "the disciple whom Jesus loved" (13:23–25; 19:26–27; 20:2–8; 21:7; 21:20–24). Then in 21:24, this "disciple whom Jesus loved" is said to be "the disciple who testifies to these things and who wrote them down."

Most scholars agree that John was the last of the four Gospels to be written. It was probably composed in A.D. 80 or 90, though estimates range from the A.D. 50s to 90s.

The theme of John's Gospel is that Jesus is the giver of life.

What was John's purpose in putting together this account of Jesus' life? Two of his statements provide the answer to this question. First, John asserts in his first epistle: "This we proclaim concerning the Word of life. The life appeared; we have seen it and testify to it... . We proclaim to you what we have seen and heard, so that you also may have fellowship with us" (1 John 1:1–3). Second, John states at the end of his Gospel: "These are written that you may believe that Jesus is the Christ, the Son of God, and that by believing you may have life in his name" (John 20:31). He tells us Jesus' story so that we will understand who Jesus is, put our faith in him as the unique Son of God, and so experience life in Christ and fellowship with other believers.

What, then, do we know about John the apostle? First, we know that he and his brother James, along with Peter and his brother Andrew, were the first four disciples called by Jesus (Mark 1:16–20). Furthermore, James and John seem inseparable. Together the two brothers want to call down fire on a village (Luke 9:54). Together they earn the title from Jesus of "Sons of Thunder" (Mark 3:17). The two of them request to be seated on Jesus' right and left in the coming kingdom (Mark 10:35–37). They are both with Jesus on the Mount of Transfiguration (Mark 9:2), in Gethsemane (Mark 14:33), and when Jairus' daughter is raised from the dead (Mark 5:37). John is right at the heart of Jesus' life and ministry. He, of all the disciples, is qualified to give the world a glimpse of Jesus' deepest thoughts and profound concerns.

For those familiar with the Synoptic Gospels (Matthew, Mark, Luke), what strikes one so forcibly about John's Gospel is how different it is. Where the Synoptic Gospels emphasize facts and historical order, John is a "right-brained" poetic writer who emphasizes meanings. Thus, he starts with a discourse on Jesus as the incarnate Word of God; he interrupts a story on Jesus and Nicodemus for the famous section on how God so loved the world that he sent his Son (3:16–17); and he includes the "I am" statements of Jesus where he defines the meaning of his coming (6:35; 8:58; 10:7,11; 14:6).

In structure, John's Gospel begins with a distinct prologue (1:1–18), and then divides into two major parts. The first part of the Gospel concentrates on Jesus' *public* ministry. It is organized around his miracles, "signs" that reveal who he really is. This part covers most of the three years of Jesus' ministry. In the second part, the focus shifts to the disciples and Jesus' *private* ministry among them. The theme in this section is the *glory* that is revealed in Jesus' crucifixion and resurrection. The time period of this part is short: from the Thursday night of the Last Supper through Jesus' post-resurrection appearances.

ICE-BREAKER   15 Min.
CONNECT WITH YOUR GROUP

LEADER

Be sure to read the introductory material in the front of this book prior to this first session. To help your group members get acquainted, have each person introduce him or herself and then take turns answering one or two of the Ice-Breaker questions. If time allows, you may want to discuss all three questions.

Today we are beginning a journey together by studying about the most important beginning that ever was or will be—that of Jesus, our light in the darkness and the Word made flesh. Take some time to get to know one another by sharing your responses to the following questions.

1. Where did you have your "beginnings"? Who was with you in the beginning? Who lived with you, and how did you get along?

2. When you were in grade school, who or what "lit up your world" when things got dark?
❏ The love of my family.
❏ The companionship of friends.
❏ My imagination.
❏ Other_____.

3. When you were in high school, if you were to choose one person to "testify" for you, to say something good about who you were and what you were about, who would it have been?

BIBLE STUDY

READ SCRIPTURE AND DISCUSS

30 Min.

LEADER

Select a member of the group ahead of time to read aloud the Scripture passage. Then discuss the Questions for Interaction, dividing into subgroups of four or five. Be sure to save time at the end for the Caring Time.

Where the other Gospel writers focus mostly on the facts of Jesus' life and ministry, right from the beginning John focuses on the *meaning* behind those facts. In the following prologue, John connects Jesus' earthly life with his eternal status as the Word, God made flesh. Read John 1:1–18 and note the beautiful way John describes Jesus.

The Word Became Flesh

1 In the beginning was the Word, and the Word was with God, and the Word was God. ²He was with God in the beginning.

³Through him all things were made; without him nothing was made that has been made. ⁴In him was life, and that life was the light of men. ⁵The light shines in the darkness, but the darkness has not understood it.

⁶There came a man who was sent from God; his name was John. ⁷He came as a witness to testify concerning that light, so that through him all men might believe. ⁸He himself was not the light; he came only as a witness to the light. ⁹The true light that gives light to every man was coming into the world.

¹⁰He was in the world, and though the world was made through him, the world did not recognize him. ¹¹He came to that which was his own, but his own did not receive him. ¹²Yet to all who received him, to those who believed in his name, he gave the right to become children of God—¹³children born not of natural descent, nor of human decision or a husband's will, but born of God.

¹⁴The Word became flesh and made his dwelling among us. We have seen his glory, the glory of the One and Only, who came from the Father, full of grace and truth.

¹⁵John testifies concerning him. He cries out, saying, "This was he of whom I said, 'He who comes after me has surpassed me because he was before me.'" ¹⁶From the fullness of his grace we have all received one blessing after another. ¹⁷For the law was given through Moses; grace and truth came through Jesus Christ. ¹⁸No one has ever seen God, but God the One and Only, who is at the Father's side, has made him known.

John 1:1–18

LEADER

Refer to the Summary and Study Notes at the end of this session as needed. If 30 minutes is not enough time to answer all of the questions in this section, conclude the Bible Study by answering question #7.

QUESTIONS FOR INTERACTION

1. What person in your life has most showed you who God is through how he or she acted and who he or she was?

2. Who is being referred to as "the Word"? Why doesn't John just use his name? What does it mean that this person is called "the Word"?

3. What does John mean when he says, "The light shines in the darkness, but the darkness has not understood it" (v. 5)? Is it still true that the darkness of the world has not "understood" the light of Jesus Christ? Where do you see this being most evident?

4. What people are given the right to become children of God? What does it mean to be a child of God?

5. According to verse 18, since we cannot see him, how can we know what God is like?

6. In what way has it been true for you, "From the fullness of his grace we have all received one blessing after another" (v. 16)?

7. In what way is darkness a part of your life right now, and what can you do to help the light of Jesus penetrate into this darkness?
  ❏ Darkness is in my own heart or spirit.
  ❏ Darkness is lurking in my future.
  ❏ There is darkness from my past that I don't quite understand.
  ❏ Darkness in the world frightens me.
  ❏ Other_____.

GOING DEEPER: *If your group has time and/or wants a challenge, go on to this question.*

8. Are not all people children of God in the sense that he created us (Acts 17:28)? How is this different than being children of God in the sense of verses 12–13 of this passage?

CARING TIME   15 Min.

APPLY THE LESSON AND PRAY FOR ONE ANOTHER

LEADER

Take some extra time in this first session to go over the introductory material at the beginning of this book. At the close, pass around your books and have everyone sign the Group Directory in the front of this book.

This very important time is for developing and expressing your concern for each other as group members by praying for one another.

1. Agree on the group covenant and ground rules (see the front of this book).

2. Recall the blessings that group members mentioned back in question #6. What blessings would you like to thank God for today?

3. Share any other prayer requests and praises, and then close in prayer. Pray specifically for God to lead you to someone to bring next week to fill the empty chair.

NEXT WEEK

Today we explored the meaning of the miracle of Jesus, the Word of God, becoming flesh. We were reminded that when we receive him we become children of God, our darkness becomes light, and our lives are filled with grace and truth. In the coming week, take some extra time each day to "dwell" with Jesus. Read John 1:1–18 again and ask Jesus to take away any darkness that remains in your life. Next week we will look at Jesus' calling of his first disciples, and see how their stories compare to our own.

NOTES ON JOHN 1:1–18

Summary: John tells us the story of Jesus Christ, as several did before him. But he is one who insists that the story does not start with a birth in a manger, an angel's announcement, or even a genealogy going back to Abraham or Adam. John's version starts before time began in the pre-existence of the Word of God, the one who we know as Jesus Christ. The Word was active in the process of creation itself. This fact makes it all the more tragic that when he came into the world to "pitch his tent among us" we didn't recognize who he was, and in fact rejected him. John makes his appeal, however, to those who have not rejected him. Such people, those who receive the Word of God in faith, are empowered to become children of God.

The greatest miracle about this truth of "the Word made flesh" is that even though we can't normally see God, we can see the Word of God as he was incarnated in Jesus Christ. That is how we can know a God who many, then and now, regard as unknowable.

1:1 *In the beginning.* This book starts with the same three words that start Genesis. Thus, we see that the coming of Jesus inaugurates a new creation (Gen. 1:1). Paul also picks up this theme of a new creation in Jesus Christ (2 Cor. 5:17; Gal. 6:15). ***the Word.*** This is the translation of the Greek word *Logos*, a word with multiple meanings. A popular form of Greek thought taught that the *Logos* was an impersonal force or principle that gave order and meaning to the universe. The Old Testament spoke of the *Logos* as the divine wisdom active in creation and human affairs (Prov. 8:12–36).

1:3 *Through him all things were made.* This connection of the Son's role in the act of creation is also made in Hebrews 1:2.

1:4 *life.* This has a double meaning, referring to both physical life and the supernatural illumination ("*the light*") that brings spiritual life to people.

1:5 *light/darkness.* This is another theme borrowed from Greek philosophy central to this Gospel's portrait of Jesus (8:12; 12:35). ***understood.*** This word also means, "over-takes" (12:35). On the one hand, the light of God shines in spite of the best effort of the powers of darkness to extinguish it. On the other hand, the widespread lack of comprehension of Jesus' identity is an important theme of this Gospel.

1:6 *John.* John the Baptist is being referred to here, not John the author of this Gospel. John the Baptist's influence was felt from Egypt to Asia Minor (Acts 18:24–26; 19:1–4).

1:8 *He himself was not the light.* There were some disciples of John the Baptist who apparently believed he was the Christ, the "light." In spite of the fact that John denied this was his role (1:20), and even pointed to Jesus as "the Lamb of God, who takes away the sin of the world" (1:29), many did not come over to him, but rather remained as disciples of John (Matt. 9:14; Luke 5:33).

1:10 *He was in the world.* This is the radically new dimension the Gospel adds to Greek or Jewish ideas about the *Logos*: it is *not* an "it," but a person! ***world.*** The first two uses of this word in this verse refer to the created order in general. The last use means humanity.

1:11 *He came to that which was his own.* Israel, God's own people (Gen. 17:7), especially failed to see who Jesus was (12:37–41).

1:12 *children of God.* Entrance into God's family is not, as orthodox Jews assumed, a natural matter of birthright or race (v. 13), but a supernatural matter of God's will based on belief in Jesus (1 John 3:1–2).

1:14 *became flesh.* This term would have shocked Greek readers who believed the flesh was so inherently worthless that the divine would have no relationship with it. They thought of spirituality as a matter of escaping the limits of the body. *made his dwelling among us.* Literally, "set his tent in us." This is an allusion to God's dwelling with Israel in the tabernacle (Ex. 33:7–11). Temporarily, God lived among people in human form. ***the One and Only.*** While Israel's kings were sometimes called "Sons of God", Jesus is God's Son in an absolutely unique sense (v. 18; 3:16,18).

1:15 *he was before me.* This is a reference to the preexistence of Christ (vv. 1–3).

1:17 *Moses/Jesus.* The grace of Jesus brings life, whereas the Law of Moses only could point out the failure of people before God. Yet Moses bore witness to Jesus; anyone who truly believed Moses would certainly receive Jesus (5:45–46). Still, this passage was essentially claiming superiority of Jesus over Moses, a claim that would have scandalized many Jews (9:28–29). Hebrews also makes this claim (Heb. 3:3–6). ***Jesus Christ.*** The incarnate *Logos* is identified for the first time. "Christ" is the Greek term for the Hebrew title "Messiah."

SESSION 2
THE FIRST DISCIPLES

SCRIPTURE   JOHN 1:35–51

LAST WEEK

In last week's session we studied the prologue to John's Gospel, which declares that Jesus is the Word made flesh and only through him can we know God. We were reminded that Jesus brings light to our darkness and makes us part of the family of God when we receive him and believe in him. This week we will learn about the calling of Jesus' first disciples, and how Jesus continues to call each one of us to do his work today.

ICE-BREAKER   15 Min.
CONNECT WITH YOUR GROUP

LEADER

Begin the session with a word of prayer. Have your group members take turns sharing their responses to one, two or all three of the Ice-Breaker questions. Be sure that everyone gets a chance to participate.

Today we will get to know Jesus better by looking at him through the eyes of the first disciples. Help others in the group get to know you better by sharing some of your unique life experiences.

1. What did you consider to be your "hometown" when you were in high school? What town or high school was your school's biggest rival?

2. What nickname do you remember having when in junior high or high school? How did you feel about that nickname?

3. When you were a child or adolescent, to whom or what did a family member introduce you?
    ❒ A special friend.
    ❒ A game or sport.
    ❒ A boyfriend or girlfriend.
    ❒ Other_____.

    Were you glad for this introduction, or did you later regret it?

BIBLE STUDY   30 Min.
READ SCRIPTURE AND DISCUSS

LEADER

Select six members of the group ahead of time to read aloud the Scripture passage. Have one member read John's narration; one member read for John the Baptist (v. 36); one member read for Andrew (vv. 38,41); one member read for Jesus (vv. 38–39,42–43,47–48, 50–51); one member read for Philip (vv. 45–46); and one member read for Nathanael (vv. 46,48–49). Then divide into subgroups of four or five and discuss the Questions for Interaction.

After being baptized by John the Baptist, Jesus goes about choosing his first disciples. Some of the stories in today's passage are unique to John. They emphasize the importance of telling others about our experience with Christ. Read John 1:35–51 and note the unique response of each disciple to the call of Jesus.

Jesus' First Disciples

John: *³⁵The next day John was there again with two of his disciples. ³⁶When he saw Jesus passing by, he said,*

John the Baptist: *"Look, the Lamb of God!"*

John: *³⁷When the two disciples heard him say this, they followed Jesus. ³⁸Turning around, Jesus saw them following and asked,*

Jesus: *"What do you want?"*

Andrew: *They said, "Rabbi" (which means Teacher), "where are you staying?"*

Jesus: *³⁹"Come," he replied, "and you will see."*

John: *So they went and saw where he was staying, and spent that day with him. It was about the tenth hour. ⁴⁰Andrew, Simon Peter's brother, was one of the two who heard what John had said and who had followed Jesus. ⁴¹The first thing Andrew did was to find his brother Simon and tell him,*

Andrew: *"We have found the Messiah"*

John: *... (that is, the Christ). ⁴²And he brought him to Jesus. Jesus looked at him and said,*

Jesus: *"You are Simon son of John. You will be called Cephas"*

John: *... (which, when translated, is Peter). ⁴³The next day Jesus decided to leave for Galilee. Finding Philip, he said to him,*

Jesus: *"Follow me."*

John: *⁴⁴Philip, like Andrew and Peter, was from the town of Bethsaida. ⁴⁵Philip found Nathanael and told him,*

Philip:	*"We have found the one Moses wrote about in the Law, and about whom the prophets also wrote—Jesus of Nazareth, the son of Joseph."*
Nathanael:	*⁴⁶"Nazareth! Can anything good come from there?" Nathanael asked.*
Philip:	*"Come and see," said Philip.*
John:	*⁴⁷When Jesus saw Nathanael approaching, he said of him,*
Jesus:	*"Here is a true Israelite, in whom there is nothing false."*
Nathanael:	*⁴⁸"How do you know me?" Nathanael asked.*
Jesus:	*Jesus answered, "I saw you while you were still under the fig tree before Philip called you."*
Nathanael:	*⁴⁹Then Nathanael declared, "Rabbi, you are the Son of God; you are the King of Israel."*
Jesus:	*⁵⁰Jesus said, "You believe because I told you I saw you under the fig tree. You shall see greater things than that." ⁵¹He then added, "I tell you the truth, you shall see heaven open, and the angels of God ascending and descending on the Son of Man."*

John 1:35–51

LEADER

Refer to the Summary and Study Notes at the end of this session as needed. If 30 minutes is not enough time to answer all of the questions in this section, conclude the Bible Study by answering question #7.

QUESTIONS FOR INTERACTION

1. Who was the mentor you "followed around" when you first started out on your own as a young adult? If this person had asked you what it was that you wanted, what would you have said?

2. When Jesus asked the two disciples what they wanted, why do you think they answered in the way that they did? What do you think it was they really wanted, and why didn't they just come out and say it?

3. What did Andrew tell his brother Simon about Jesus? What do you think convinced him that this was true?

4. What seems to be Nathanael's attitude about Nazareth? What do you think is behind this negative attitude? What turns this attitude around in relation to his opinion of Jesus?

5. What does Jesus say about Nathanael? Do you think he was aware of Nathanael's negative attitude about Nazareth and people who come from there?

6. If Jesus turned to you today and asked, "What do you want?" how would you respond?

7. Nathanael believed because Jesus seemed to know so much about him before they even met. What has brought *you* to believe in Jesus? What "greater things than that" have you experienced since your conversion that have helped to solidify your belief?

GOING DEEPER: *If your group has time and/or wants a challenge, go on to this question.*

8. What do you see as the keys to the effectiveness of Andrew and Philip in telling their brother and friend, respectively, about Jesus?

CARING TIME   15 Min.
APPLY THE LESSON AND PRAY FOR ONE ANOTHER

LEADER

Bring the group members back together and begin the Caring Time by sharing responses to all three questions. Then share prayer requests and praises. Be sure to take turns so everyone gets a chance to participate.

Take some time now to encourage and support one another in a time of sharing and prayer. Remember the disciples helped each other to follow the call of Jesus.

1. What Simon* (person in your family) or Nathanael* (friend or acquaintance) could you invite to this group to "come and see"? How can this group pray for this person in advance?

2. How can this group pray for you in relation to what you shared in question #6 (what you want from Jesus)?

3. Take time to thank God for those "greater things" (question #7) that you have experienced.

*We use these male names because they are in the text, but that does not preclude including women!

P. S. *Add new group members to the Group Directory at the beginning of this book.*

NEXT WEEK

Today we looked at the calling of Jesus' disciples, and how they each responded to Jesus in their own unique way. In the coming week, keep praying for the person you would like to invite to the group, and do some act of kindness such as inviting him or her over for dinner. Next week we will consider Jesus' first miracle, the turning of water into wine at Cana. We will also consider what relevance this miracle has to the rest of his ministry.

NOTES ON JOHN 1:35–51

Summary: John now switches from his more philosophical prologue to an historical account of Jesus' selection of his first disciples. The interesting thing here is that Jesus does not directly recruit some of them, as seems most commonly the case in the synoptics (Matt. 9:9; Mark 1:16–17,19–20), but the new disciples go out and recruit other disciples. In these stories, then, are some of our best examples of evangelism—telling someone else what we have experienced in Jesus Christ. Andrew brought his brother Peter, while Philip went out and recruited his friend Nathanael.

Nathanael voices his doubts that anything good can come out of Nazareth, but those doubts are quickly answered when he finds that this person from Nazareth has a supernatural kind of knowledge about him. Jesus promises he will see and experience "greater things than that."

1:35 *John.* This is John the Baptist, not the apostle John who wrote this Gospel.

1:36 *the Lamb of God.* This means the one who God would use as a sacrifice for sin. Such sacrifices, according to Old Testament Law, were to be flawless lambs (Lev. 1:10).

1:38 *What do you want?* The motivation of those who would follow him is a concern for Jesus (2:24; 6:26). ***Rabbi.*** Rabbis were teachers who gathered disciples around them. ***staying.*** This is the same word translated in verse 33 as "remain."

1:39 *Come ... and you will see.* Jesus invites these followers to enter into the journey of discipleship with him. He invites them to experience who he is and where they are going for themselves. In a similar way, Philip later invites Nathanael to "Come and see." ***the tenth hour.*** Time was measured from the first light of day. Since daybreak was about 6 A.M., this was about 4 P.M.

1:41 *We have found the Messiah.* This is the fourth title ascribed to Jesus in this section (vv. 29–38). The Messiah is the "anointed one" or the special king sent from God to redeem Israel (all of Israel's kings were anointed).

1:42 *Cephas.* The Aramaic name Cephas and the Greek name Peter both mean "rock." Although Peter often seemed unstable during

23

Jesus' time with him (18:15–17,25–27), after the Ascension Peter became the chief spokesman for the apostles and was later a leader in the early church (Acts 2:14).

1:43 *Galilee.* Galilee, where Jesus was raised, was a province 60 miles north of Jerusalem. One of the reasons the Pharisees rejected Jesus' claim to messiahship was because they assumed he was born in Galilee (7:41,52).

1:45 *Moses wrote about in the Law.* This refers to the Prophet to come (Deut. 18:18), the fulfillment of the Old Testament hope (1:21).

1:46 *Nazareth!* This was a small, insignificant village in Galilee. It seemed impossible to Nathanael that the one Philip described could come from such a place. His incredulity may stem either from the fact that this was a nearby town with which he was familiar (Jesus noted that "a prophet has no honor in his own country"—4:44), or perhaps it was a rival town to Nathanael's own hometown of Cana (21:2).

1:47 *a true Israelite.* "Israel" was the name given to Jacob after he wrestled with an angel, but his previous name of "Jacob" meant "supplanter." The name recalls his father Isaac's complaint, "Your brother came deceitfully and took your blessing" (Gen. 27:35). In contrast, Nathanael is an Israelite in whom, unlike their ancestor, there was nothing false or deceitful.

1:48 *How do you know me?* This is not the only incident in this Gospel of someone being impressed with how completely Jesus knows them. The woman at the well told her Samaritan acquaintances, "Come, see a man who told me everything I ever did" (4:29). ***I saw you.*** This accents the supernatural knowledge of Jesus, which is part of what impresses Nathanael that this man is the Son of God. Also, for him to say that he saw Nathanael while he was still under the fig tree was to say that he saw him when he made the cynical remark about anything good coming out of Nazareth. This may have been a subtle message to Nathanael about stereotyping.

1:50 *greater things.* This is probably an illusion to the miracles Jesus will perform as signs of his divine identity, culminated by the grand miracle of his resurrection.

1:51 This recalls Jacob's dream (Gen. 28:10–22), with the significant difference that Jesus replaces the ladder as the means of communication between heaven and earth. The new Bethel (house of God—Gen. 28:19) is found in Jesus himself. ***the Son of Man.*** Of all the titles for Jesus in this chapter, this is the one he uses for himself. Daniel 7:13ff provides its background as the one invested with divine authority to rule the earth, but it was not a commonly used term for the Messiah in Jesus' time.

SESSION 3
JESUS' FIRST MIRACLE

SCRIPTURE   JOHN 2:1–11

LAST WEEK

In our previous session we considered the calling of Jesus' first disciples, and the role that evangelism played in that calling. We were reminded that Jesus still calls us today to ask others to "come and see." This week we will examine Jesus' first miracle, the turning of water into wine at Cana, and we will consider the meaning of that miracle for Jesus' ministry. We will also discuss how Jesus continues today to take ordinary people ("water") and change us into new and exciting creations ("wine").

ICE-BREAKER   15 Min.
CONNECT WITH YOUR GROUP

LEADER

Begin the session with prayer, asking God for his blessing and presence. Choose one or two Ice-Breaker questions. If you have a new group member you may want to do all three. Remember to stick closely to the three-part agenda and the time allowed for each segment.

Jesus took part in all of the ordinary experiences of life, as well as its great celebrations. Take turns sharing your thoughts about some of those experiences in your life.

1. When you were in high school, what was your mother most likely to try to get you to do that you didn't want to do? How did you react to her demands?

2. What was the most elaborate wedding you have ever attended? What about the ceremony or reception impressed you the most?

3. What makes a party a "real party" for you?
    ❐ The food and drink.
    ❐ Planned activities.
    ❐ Having someone around who is "the life of the party."
    ❐ Just relaxing with good friends.
    ❐ Other_____.

BIBLE STUDY

READ SCRIPTURE AND DISCUSS

30 Min.

LEADER

Have a member of the group, selected ahead of time, read aloud the Scripture passage. Then discuss the Questions for Interaction, dividing into smaller subgroups of four or five.

In our story for this week, Jesus attends a wedding along with his disciples. In the course of this event, his mother asks him to help the host avoid a social faux pas by making more wine after they had unexpectedly run out. Next to healing the sick and raising the dead, this seems like a relatively trivial place to begin. But if we really consider the story, we can see it all had a bigger importance than it initially might seem. Read John 2:1–11 and note the results of Jesus' first miracle.

Jesus Changes Water to Wine

2 On the third day a wedding took place at Cana in Galilee. Jesus' mother was there, ²and Jesus and his disciples had also been invited to the wedding. ³When the wine was gone, Jesus' mother said to him, "They have no more wine."

⁴"Dear woman, why do you involve me?" Jesus replied, "My time has not yet come."

⁵His mother said to the servants, "Do whatever he tells you."

⁶Nearby stood six stone water jars, the kind used by the Jews for ceremonial washing, each holding from twenty to thirty gallons.

⁷Jesus said to the servants, "Fill the jars with water"; so they filled them to the brim.

⁸Then he told them, "Now draw some out and take it to the master of the banquet."

They did so, ⁹and the master of the banquet tasted the water that had been turned into wine. He did not realize where it had come from, though the servants who had drawn the water knew. Then he called the bridegroom aside ¹⁰and said, "Everyone brings out the choice wine first and then the cheaper wine after the guests have had too much to drink; but you have saved the best till now."

¹¹This, the first of his miraculous signs, Jesus performed at Cana in Galilee. He thus revealed his glory, and his disciples put their faith in him.

John 2:1–11

QUESTIONS FOR INTERACTION

1. Had your own mother been in the place of Mary, how would she have behaved?
   ❐ Avoided a party with wine altogether.
   ❐ Stayed out of the matter.
   ❐ Been equally persistent as Mary.
   ❐ Other_____.

2. Why does Jesus respond to his mother in the way that he does? Why does he go ahead and produce the wine in spite of his initial objection to getting involved?

3. Approximately how much water was turned into wine? Why do you suppose he made so much? (See the Summary in the "Notes" section for one possibility.)

4. Why is the master of the banquet so surprised at the quality of the wine that Jesus miraculously produced from water? How did serving such wine run counter to what was traditionally done?

5. What does verse 11 say was the end result of this miracle?

6. In what ways has Jesus "turned water into wine" in your life? – taken the common and ordinary and made it into something special?

7. What are you running out of right now that you would like Jesus to restore?
   ❐ My energy level.
   ❐ My faith in the future.
   ❐ My joy for life.
   ❐ My sense of connection with others.
   ❐ Other_____.

GOING DEEPER: *If your group has time and/or wants a challenge, go on to this question.*

8. Jesus apparently didn't want to start his ministry with this miracle, but he did because of the insistence of his mother. What does this say about Jesus' (and God's) flexibility in carrying out his plans?

CARING TIME   15 Min.

APPLY THE LESSON AND PRAY FOR ONE ANOTHER

LEADER

Begin the Caring Time by having group members take turns sharing responses to all three questions. Be sure to save at least the last five minutes for a time of group prayer. Remember to include a prayer for the empty chair when concluding the prayer time.

As Mary asked Jesus for help at the wedding, go now to Jesus and ask him for help with all of your needs and the needs of other group members. Remember that this time is for encouraging and supporting one another through sharing and prayer requests.

1. How is your relationship with Jesus right now?
  ❏ Close.
  ❏ Improving.
  ❏ Strained.
  ❏ Growing apart.
  ❏ Other_____.

2. What miracle would you like to ask Jesus for today?

3. How can this group pray for you in connection with the shortage you reported in question #7 under the Questions for Interaction?

NEXT WEEK

Today we looked at Jesus' first miracle at Cana, and how it "revealed his glory, and his disciples put their faith in him" (v. 11). In the coming week, let Jesus work a miracle through you by helping someone in a difficult situation. Next week we will look at the story of a religious leader named Nicodemus who came to Jesus with some searching questions. We will listen in as Jesus gently teaches him about spiritual birth.

NOTES ON JOHN 2:1–11

Summary: Here is a story that helps us to see that Jesus enjoyed the great celebrations of life just as we do. He wasn't intending to start his public ministry with this miracle in Cana, but rather he was there to just celebrate with a friend. However, because of his desire to respond to a request by his mother, he modified his plans. To help the hosts avoid embarrassment he turned from 120 to 180 gallons of water into wine!

Of what importance is this miracle, other than to show Jesus' responsiveness to his mother? As a miracle, isn't it a little trivial when compared to his later miracles of healing the sick and raising people from the dead? One can look at this miracle, however, as having significant symbolic value. Jesus later compared his blood to wine "poured out for many" (Matt. 26:28). If indeed Jesus had decided to make this miracle a symbolic statement, this would make it a little more understandable as to why Jesus produced so much wine, enough to supply many weddings! Thus, this miracle is similar in meaning to when Jesus multiplied the loaves and fishes to provide for many (6:1–15), a miracle that spoke of the sufficiency of his sacrifice for the multitudes.

2:1 *a wedding took place.* A wedding was a week-long feast. Jesus' presence here reminds us that he was not a dour-faced ascetic who avoided the celebrations of life. ***at Cana.*** The exact location of this village is unknown, but it is believed to have been near Nazareth.

2:3 *When the wine was gone.* This was a humiliating social situation. It would reflect badly on the host as someone too miserly to provide adequate refreshments for the guests. ***Jesus' mother.*** Mary plays a minor role in this Gospel, appearing only here and in 19:25–27. Her concern for the situation as well as her relationship to the servants (v. 5) indicates she may have been active in the planning of the wedding.

2:6 *used by the Jews for ceremonial washing.* See Mark 7:3–4. This was not washing to cleanse hands of germs, but rather part of a religious purification rite.

2:8 *the master of the banquet.* This appears to be an honored guest at the wedding, serving in a role somewhat similar to that of a modern-day toastmaster.

2:10 *Everyone brings out the choice wine first.* Typically, the best wine would be served when the guests would be most able to appreciate it. Later on, when they are less likely to notice, a cheaper quality of wine would be introduced. The quality of this wine was such that the bridegroom was praised for bringing out the best last.

2:11 *miraculous signs.* John uses this term frequently to describe Jesus' miracles in order to encourage his readers not to see them simply as acts of power, but as pointers to God's presence in Jesus seen by those who receive him (1:12). Likewise, they are physical and material illustrations of the spiritual life Jesus came to bring (6:26–27; 9:1–5,39). ***glory.*** In this action, the disciples saw their first glimpse of the light of God's glory manifested in Jesus (1:14), seen in the hue of his ability to transform a dismal situation into one of richness and abundance.

29

SESSION 4
JESUS TEACHES NICODEMUS

SCRIPTURE JOHN 3:1–21

LAST WEEK

In last week's session we considered Jesus' first miracle, the turning of water into wine at Cana. We saw how this revealed his glory to the disciples and strengthened their faith. We also considered how today Jesus continues to take the common and ordinary and turn it into something special. This week we will look at some of his teachings, which are shared through an encounter with Nicodemus, a member of the Jewish ruling council. We will especially address Jesus' teaching on what it means to be "born again."

ICE-BREAKER   15 Min.
CONNECT WITH YOUR GROUP

LEADER

Choose one, two or all three of the Ice-Breaker questions. Welcome and introduce new group members and begin with a word of prayer.

There are many universal life experiences that we all share and can relate to. Jesus often used "earthly things" to illustrate his teachings and help us to understand "heavenly things." Take turns sharing some of your "earthly" experiences.

1. Where were you born? What have your parents told you about any unusual circumstances (special challenges, people who came to visit, etc.) surrounding your birth?

2. Apart from any conversion experience, what is the closest you have come to feeling like you had been reborn?
    ❏ When I met a new romantic interest or got remarried.
    ❏ When I found an exciting new job.
    ❏ When I was healed of a disease or had surgery.
    ❏ Other_____.

3. What is your favorite activity to do in relation to the wind?
- ❏ Fly a kite.
- ❏ Wind surf.
- ❏ Stay in a warm house and listen to it howl.
- ❏ Other_____.

BIBLE STUDY   30 Min.
READ SCRIPTURE AND DISCUSS

LEADER

Ask three group members, selected ahead of time, to read aloud the Scripture passage. Have one person read John's narration; another read the part of Nicodemus (vv. 2,4,9); and the third read the part of Jesus (vv. 3,5–8,10–21). Then discuss the Questions for Interaction, dividing into subgroups of four or five. Be sure to save at least 15–20 minutes at the end for the Caring Time.

Even though the Pharisees often rejected Jesus' teaching and authority and gave him a hard time, John includes this story about a Pharisee named Nicodemus who comes to Jesus earnestly seeking spiritual truth. Read John 3:1–21 and note how Jesus explains what it means to be spiritually reborn.

Jesus Teaches Nicodemus

John:	*Now there was a man of the Pharisees named Nicodemus, a member of the Jewish ruling council. ²He came to Jesus at night and said,*
Nicodemus:	*"Rabbi, we know you are a teacher who has come from God. For no one could perform the miraculous signs you are doing if God were not with him."*
Jesus:	*3In reply Jesus declared, "I tell you the truth, no one can see the kingdom of God unless he is born again."*
Nicodemus:	*⁴"How can a man be born when he is old?" Nicodemus asked. "Surely he cannot enter a second time into his mother's womb to be born!"*

Jesus: *⁵Jesus answered, "I tell you the truth, no one can enter the kingdom of God unless he is born of water and the Spirit. ⁶Flesh gives birth to flesh, but the Spirit gives birth to spirit. ⁷You should not be surprised at my saying, 'You must be born again.' ⁸The wind blows wherever it pleases. You hear its sound, but you cannot tell where it comes from or where it is going. So it is with everyone born of the Spirit."*

Nicodemus: *⁹"How can this be?" Nicodemus asked.*

Jesus: *¹⁰"You are Israel's teacher," said Jesus, "and you do not understand these things? ¹¹I tell you the truth, we speak of what we know, and we testify to what we have seen, but still you people do not accept our testimony. ¹²I have spoken to you of earthly things and you do not believe; how then will you believe if I speak of heavenly things? ¹³No one has ever gone into heaven except the one who came from heaven—the Son of Man. ¹⁴Just as Moses lifted up the snake in the desert, so the Son of Man must be lifted up, ¹⁵that everyone who believes in him may have eternal life.*

¹⁶"For God so loved the world that he gave his one and only Son, that whoever believes in him shall not perish but have eternal life. ¹⁷For God did not send his Son into the world to condemn the world, but to save the world through him. ¹⁸Whoever believes in him is not condemned, but whoever does not believe stands condemned already because he has not believed in the name of God's one and only Son. ¹⁹This is the verdict: Light has come into the world, but men loved darkness instead of light because their deeds were evil. ²⁰Everyone who does evil hates the light, and will not come into the light for fear that his deeds will be exposed. ²¹But whoever lives by the truth comes into the light, so that it may be seen plainly that what he has done has been done through God."

John 3:1–21

LEADER

Refer to the Summary and Study Notes at the end of the session as needed. If 30 minutes is not enough time to answer all of the questions in this section, conclude the Bible Study by answering questions #7 and #8.

QUESTIONS FOR INTERACTION

1. Why does Nicodemus believe that Jesus is "a teacher who has come from God" (v. 2)? Why does he start off their conversation with this statement?

2. Had Jesus asked Nicodemus the question he asked of the disciples in 1:38, "What do you want?" what do you think he would have answered?

3. What does Jesus say a person must do in order to see the kingdom of God? What does he say later in order to clarify the meaning of this requirement? Is the phrase in the question more or less clear to you than it was to Nicodemus?

4. What did Jesus do that was like Moses lifting up the snake in the wilderness (see note on v. 14)? How does verse 16 shed further light on this?

5. Why does Jesus especially point out that God didn't send him into the world to condemn the world? If this is the case, then why do some people end up being condemned anyway?

6. Who is the light referred to in verse 19? Why do some people avoid this light?

7. How much light do you feel you are seeing in your own spiritual life right now?
❒ Like on a bright, sunny day.
❒ Like on an overcast day.
❒ Like early dawn.
❒ Like the darkest cave where no light enters.

8. What do you need to do right now in order to let more light into your life?

 GOING DEEPER: *If your group has time and/or wants a challenge, go on to this question.*

9. Why do some people seem to love the darkness?
❒ Because they are used to it.
❒ Because they haven't been taught any better.
❒ Because they are ashamed.
❒ Other_____.

What can a Christian do to help such a person not just "see the light," but also see the *benefit* of more light in his or her life?

❤ CARING TIME   15 Min.
APPLY THE LESSON AND PRAY FOR ONE ANOTHER

LEADER

Be sure to save at least 15 minutes for this important time. After sharing responses to all three questions and asking for prayer requests, close in a time of group prayer.

Once again, take some time now to show God's love to one another by sharing your responses to the following questions and praying for each other.

1. Where are you right now in the birthing and growing process of spiritual life?
❒ Not yet conceived.
❒ Developing, but not so anyone could tell.
❒ Heavy with child and waiting.
❒ Kicking and screaming like an infant.
❒ Growing daily.

2. How has this group been a source of light in the darkness to you? What would you like to say to thank God for that light?

3. In what area or areas of your life do you need a rebirth right now? How can the group help you with this through prayer?

NEXT WEEK

Today we considered the story of Nicodemus and his confusion about what it means to be "born again." We saw how Jesus emphasized God's love for humanity, not his condemnation. In the coming week, share God's love in some way with a person who is skeptical of your faith. Next week we will learn more from Jesus as he encounters a woman who had experienced much rejection in her lifetime, in part because of ethnic reasons and in part because of her lifestyle. We will see what Jesus' response to her means for us as we go through similar struggles.

NOTES ON JOHN 3:1–21

Summary: Sometimes we don't know how to ask our deepest questions. That may have been the case with Nicodemus as he came to Jesus on that night long ago. As it turned out, Nicodemus didn't have to ask his question—Jesus already knew it. Nicodemus, although a religious leader of his day, felt a need for spiritual renewal, and he didn't know how to find it. Jesus told him that he had to be born again. We hear the phrase all of the time. But it was new to Nicodemus, and he didn't know how to take it.

Jesus explained by saying that one had to do more than be born physically. One also has to be born of the Spirit. Jesus' purpose in coming into the world was to help that transformation happen. Any person who believed in him would never perish, but would live eternally. To those who received the light of who he was, it would indeed mean a spiritual rebirth.

3:1 *Pharisees.* Judaism was divided into various sects along doctrinal, political, practical and social lines. The Pharisees were committed to the principle that religious and ethical purity was the means of securing God's favor. ***Nicodemus.*** Nicodemus, a respected religious authority (v. 10), appears in John 7:50 and 19:39, but in no other Gospel. While he may have come to Jesus at night because of a desire to keep his interest in Jesus relatively secret, in these other stories he is more outspoken and active in his discipleship. **Jewish ruling council.** This was the Sanhedrin—the religious and political governing body of Judea. Comprised of 71 members and presided over by the high priest, its self-perpetuating membership included priests, elders and scribes.

3:3 born again. This phrase can be translated in two ways—"born again" or "born from above." The former highlights the radical reorientation to life resulting from trusting Jesus while the latter accents the reality that spiritual life is a gift from God, not something earned by virtue of one's performance (1:12–13).

3:5 born of water and the Spirit. Commentators differ on what is meant here: (1) Some think this phrase is a restatement of the call for a spiritual birth in addition to a physical birth (v. 3); (2) Others assume water illustrates the life-giving qualities of the Spirit (7:38–39); and (3) Others see this as teaching that two kinds of baptism are necessary for spiritual regeneration—water baptism and baptism of the Spirit.

3:8 The wind blows. The Greek word for "wind" and "spirit" is the same word—*pneuma*. Jesus uses this to point out an important similarity between the wind and those led by the Spirit. Those led by the Spirit are led by a force full of mystery, and one cannot always know in advance where the Holy Spirit might lead.

3:13 This Gospel's witness to Jesus is from the perspective of the whole story already told, hence the author can refer to the ascension of Jesus even at this point.

3:14 Because of rebellion, God sent deadly serpents into the midst of the Israelites during their time in the wilderness. When they called for mercy, God instructed Moses to put up on a pole a statue of a serpent. Whoever looked upon the statue would not die

(Num. 21:4–9). In a similar way, when people look with faith upon Jesus who is "lifted up" (another double-edged phrase referring to his crucifixion and resurrection/ascension), their judgment is averted and they are brought into life (6:40).

3:15 eternal life. This is the first use of a phrase seen over and over in this Gospel. Its meaning is not simply tied up with the quantity of time one exists, but with the quality of life, a quality of fullness, goodness and perfection of life with God.

3:16 God so loved the world. This is the great motivation behind God's plan of salvation (1 John 4:9–10). The popularity of this Bible verse is due to its two positive declarations: (1) God loves us so much that he gave his all—the gift of his own Son, and (2) life does not end in *perishing* for those who have faith. **he gave.** This is evidenced especially in the act of Jesus' incarnation and crucifixion.

3:17 not ... to condemn the world. Some see the Christian religion as essentially a religion of condemnation. This is a strong assertion that such is not the way it is to be. Jesus did not come to condemn, but to save. **to save the world.** The whole point of Jesus' mission was to provide all people with access to God.

3:18 condemned already. It is our own behavior that condemns us. Through Jesus, God is seeking to save us from the condemnation that is the result of our own actions. **one and only Son.** In one sense, all who are obedient to God are children of God (Rom. 8:14; 9:26; 2 Cor. 6:16–18; Gal. 3:26; 4:4–7; Eph. 1:5; Phil. 2:14–15; Heb. 12:5–9). However, Jesus is the unique Son of God, in that he fully reflects the Father.

3:19–20 Just as John 3:16–18 sums up the good news of the Gospel, so these verses sum up the human situation that makes the

Gospel so necessary. The problem is not a lack of understanding of the "light," but a decided preference for the "darkness." This point is echoed in Romans 1:18, where Paul speaks of people suppressing the truth of God in order to pursue a life of sin and wickedness.

3:21 *whoever lives by the truth.* This stands in parallel with "whoever believes in him" (v. 16) and in contrast with "everyone who does evil" (v. 20). Taken together, these phrases show that belief in Jesus and a lifestyle marked by obedience to God's ways go hand in hand (1 John 3:10).

Session 5
Jesus Talks with a Samaritan Woman

Scripture John 4:4–30,39–42

LAST WEEK

As we listened in last week on the conversation between Jesus and the Pharisee, Nicodemus, we were reminded of what it means to be spiritually "born again." We were also reminded of the unconditional love that God has for us, and how he wants so much to bring light into our darkness. This week we will look at an encounter Jesus has with a woman of the hated Samaritan culture, and see how he responds to her with great love and compassion.

ICE-BREAKER   15 Min.
Connect With Your Group

LEADER

Begin the session with prayer, asking God for his blessing and presence. To help new group members get acquainted, remember to do all three Ice-Breaker questions.

God has a plan for each person he creates (even the Samaritan woman in today's story), and each person is a unique, one-of-a-kind individual. Take turns responding to the following questions and share what makes you unique.

1. What do you have that was passed down to you from your ancestors? How did you come to have it, and what do you feel about having it?

2. Who do you have the hardest time asking for a favor?
    ❑ My parents or my spouse.
    ❑ Friends.
    ❑ Neighbors.
    ❑ Other_____.

    What makes it hard for you?

3. Where do you find it easier to worship God?

❏ In a small, intimate chapel.

❏ In a magnificent cathedral.

❏ In the mountains.

❏ On an ocean side beach.

BIBLE STUDY   30 Min.
READ SCRIPTURE AND DISCUSS

LEADER

Have a member of the group, selected ahead of time, read aloud the Scripture passage. Then discuss the Questions for Interaction, dividing into smaller subgroups of four or five.

Jesus often reached out to people who were beyond the normal "comfort zone" of most Jewish rabbis. In the following story he talks to a Samaritan woman, even though most Jewish rabbis would have not talked to her, both because she was a woman and because she was a Samaritan, a culture they hated. Jesus' combination of gentleness and spiritual insight wins over not only her, but many in her village as well.

Jesus Talks With a Samaritan Woman

4 Now he had to go through Samaria. ⁵So he came to a town in Samaria called Sychar, near the plot of ground Jacob had given to his son Joseph. ⁶Jacob's well was there, and Jesus, tired as he was from the journey, sat down by the well. It was about the sixth hour.

⁷When a Samaritan woman came to draw water, Jesus said to her, "Will you give me a drink?" ⁸(His disciples had gone into the town to buy food.)

⁹The Samaritan woman said to him, "You are a Jew and I am a Samaritan woman. How can you ask me for a drink?" (For Jews do not associate with Samaritans.)

¹⁰Jesus answered her, "If you knew the gift of God and who it is that asks you for a drink, you would have asked him and he would have given you living water."

¹¹"Sir," the woman said, "you have nothing to draw with and the well is deep. Where can you get this living water? ¹²Are you greater than our father Jacob, who gave us the well and drank from it himself, as did also his sons and his flocks and herds?"

¹³Jesus answered, "Everyone who drinks this water will be thirsty again, ¹⁴but whoever drinks the water I give him will never thirst. Indeed, the water I give him will become in him a spring of water welling up to eternal life."

¹⁵The woman said to him, "Sir, give me this water so that I won't get thirsty and have to keep coming here to draw water."

¹⁶He told her, "Go, call your husband and come back."

¹⁷"I have no husband," she replied.

Jesus said to her, "You are right when you say you have no husband. ¹⁸The fact is, you have had five husbands, and the man you now have is not your husband. What you have just said is quite true."

¹⁹"Sir," the woman said, "I can see that you are a prophet. ²⁰Our fathers worshiped on this mountain, but you Jews claim that the place where we must worship is in Jerusalem."

²¹Jesus declared, "Believe me, woman, a time is coming when you will worship the Father neither on this mountain nor in Jerusalem. ²²You Samaritans worship what you do not know; we worship what we do know, for salvation is from the Jews. ²³Yet a time is coming and has now come when the true worshipers will worship the Father in spirit and truth, for they are the kind of worshipers the Father seeks. ²⁴God is spirit, and his worshipers must worship in spirit and in truth."

²⁵The woman said, "I know that Messiah" (called Christ) "is coming. When he comes, he will explain everything to us."

²⁶Then Jesus declared, "I who speak to you am he."

²⁷Just then his disciples returned and were surprised to find him talking with a woman. But no one asked, "What do you want?" or "Why are you talking with her?"

²⁸Then, leaving her water jar, the woman went back to the town and said to the people, ²⁹"Come, see a man who told me everything I ever did. Could this be the Christ?" ³⁰They came out of the town and made their way toward him. ...

³⁹Many of the Samaritans from that town believed in him because of the woman's testimony, "He told me everything I ever did." ⁴⁰So when the Samaritans came to him, they urged him to stay with them, and he stayed two days. ⁴¹And because of his words many more became believers.

⁴²They said to the woman, "We no longer believe just because of what you said; now we have heard for ourselves, and we know that this man really is the Savior of the world."

John 4:4–30,39–42

QUESTIONS FOR INTERACTION

LEADER

Refer to the Summary and Study Notes at the end of this session as needed. If 30 minutes is not enough time to answer all of the questions in this section, conclude the Bible Study by answering question #7.

1. What group of people is for you what the Samaritans were for the Jews—a group that you don't understand and even feel an aversion for?

❒ People of a different race.

❒ The homeless.

❒ Young people in Gothic dress.

❒ Other_____.

2. When you meet someone new are you more like the Samaritan woman, cautious and protective; or like Jesus, outgoing and vulnerable?

3. What is Jesus offering this woman when he offers her "living water"? Why does she take so long to figure out what he is saying with this image?

4. How do you think the Samaritan woman felt when Jesus revealed that he knew about her five husbands? Why did he make a point of showing that he knew this?

5. How does Jesus respond to the woman's question about the proper place to worship? What does he mean when he says that we must worship God "in spirit and in truth"?

6. What makes this woman think that Jesus might indeed be the Christ? What helps many of her fellow townspeople come to the same conclusion?

7. What have you experienced for yourself that has convinced you that Jesus is the Christ, sent from God?

GOING DEEPER: *If your group has time and/or wants a challenge, go on to this question.*

8. What do we need to do to get past cultural divisions today, divisions like the one between the Jews and the Samaritans? What can we learn from how Jesus related to this woman about relating to someone of a different culture?

CARING TIME 15 Min.
APPLY THE LESSON AND PRAY FOR ONE ANOTHER

Take some time now to support and encourage one another, as Jesus supported and cared for the Samaritan woman. Begin by sharing your responses to the questions below. Conclude by sharing prayer requests and praying for each other's needs.

1. What division in the world would you like the group to pray for today?

2. What are you "thirsting for" at this time in your life? How can the group help you in prayer regarding that thirst?

3. Who has come into your life and, like Jesus, listened to you and cared for you? What about this person would you like to thank God for in prayer?

NEXT WEEK

Today we discussed the encounter Jesus had with the Samaritan woman. We saw how his compassion and mercy transcended the ethnic and moral barriers existing between them. In the coming week, step out of your "comfort zone" and reach out to someone from the group you mentioned in question #1 under the Questions for Interaction. Next week we will consider another one of Jesus' miracles as he heals a man who had been an invalid for 38 years, and look at what it means for our own healing.

NOTES ON JOHN 4:4–30, 39–42

Summary: Last week we studied Jesus' encounter with a highly respected Jewish man, Nicodemus. In contrast, today's story goes in the exact opposite direction. Here Jesus encounters a person who would have had virtually no respect. She was a Samaritan, a half-breed race despised by pious Jews. As a woman she was also looked down upon by a society that did not value women. To make things even worse, she was a woman with a bad reputation, since she had been married five times and now was living with a man to whom she was not married. But Jesus shows his acceptance of her by talking to her, and by asking her for a drink.

To ask someone for something is actually a compliment. It is saying, "I need you." To give someone a chance to give to you is to open up the relationship. Just like there is a problem when people can only receive, there is also a problem when people know only how to give. Those who do not know how to receive from others are saying they can only be in the superior position of the one doing the giving, and that can make the other person feel inadequate. Jesus wisely provides the opportunity to let this woman give to him. But then he goes on to show what he has to offer her—living water to restore her injured spirit. He also shows that even though he knows "the skeletons in her closet" he loves and accepts her. This is an important part of why she comes to believe his claim that he is the Messiah.

4:4 *Samaria.* This was a territory sandwiched between the provinces of Judea and Galilee. When the Assyrians conquered the northern kingdom of Israel in 722 B.C., many of its people were deported, and exiles from other areas of the vast Assyrian Empire were brought in (2 Kings 17:22–41). Many of these people intermarried with the remaining Israelites and adopted some of the Jewish religious practices. This created a mixed race that was despised by purebred Jews. In Jesus' day, strict Jews would avoid Samaria as an unclean area, and the term "Samaritan" was used as an insult (8:48).

4:5 *near the plot of ground Jacob had given to his son Joseph.* Genesis 48:22 tells of Jacob giving some land to Joseph.

4:6 *the sixth hour.* Since the day began at sunrise, about six in the morning, this is about noon.

4:7 *came to draw water.* Noontime, in the heat of the day, was not the normal time women would perform this chore. She was avoiding conversation with other women, which implies she received their criticism.

4:9 *Jews do not associate with Samaritans.* Since some strands of Judaism regarded Samaritans as unclean from birth, Jesus' request shocks this woman. It is also significant that she is a *woman.* It would be considered scandalous for a rabbi to talk with a strange woman.

4:10 *living water.* This was a common phrase meaning water that flowed from a river or spring. Water like this had better quality than the standing water of a well or pond. Jesus, however, is giving the phrase a new meaning, as in "water that brings life to the spirit."

4:14 *spring.* This is the same word translated as "well" (v. 6). By this play on words the author presents us with a picture of two fountains or wells. Jesus' "well" forever quenches spiritual thirst simply for the asking.

4:17–18 While clearly revealing his knowledge of her situation, Jesus commends her truthfulness. Women in this time could be divorced for trivial reasons, but had no right of divorce themselves. Still, she would have been considered undesirable and immoral, which is probably why she had come to the well at a time when other women would not be there. It is significant what Jesus does

not do—lecture her or condemn her for her past. The fact that he is talking to her even though he knows about her life shows he accepts her. Religious men would normally be expected to avoid contact with such women (Luke 7:36–50).

4:19 *prophet.* Jesus' knowledge of her led her to see him as a prophet who must be taken seriously.

4:21–23 In John 2:12–22 Jesus had shown that he himself is the new temple that supersedes the physical building in Jerusalem. Here he shows that his appearing likewise supersedes the Samaritan religious claims. The point is not where one worships, but whom.

4:23 *a time is coming and has now come.* This captures the tension of the Gospel's announcement about the kingdom of God. It is both present and yet future. *true worshipers.* The barrier between Jewish and Samaritan religion is dismissed. Their concern about location indicates that both have missed the point.

4:24 *God is spirit, and his worshipers must worship in spirit and in truth.* That God is spirit is one of three affirmations that John makes about God's nature. In 1 John 1:5 he tells us "God is light." In 1 John 4:8, he tells us "God is love." Here he tells us "God is spirit." What implication does the fact that God is spirit have for worship? Certainly one who is spirit cannot be limited to a building, like the temple (Acts 17:24), or to being on a mountain (vv. 19–21).

4:27 *surprised to find him talking to a woman.* See note on verse 9.

4:29 *Come, see.* This is the same invitation to discipleship extended to Andrew and Nathanael (1:39–40,46). *Could this be the Christ?* The phrase in Greek appears to require a negative answer, yet hopes for a positive one.

4:40 *he stayed two days.* Pious Jews were not supposed to travel through Samaria, much less stay in a Samaritan's home! This showed Jesus' acceptance of the Samaritans.

4:42 *We no longer believe just because of what you said.* This is the transformation that every believer must eventually make—conversion from belief because of someone else's experience (a parent or spiritual mentor) to one's own experience. It parallels the experience of Job who said, "My ears had heard of you but now my eyes have seen you" (Job 42:5). ***Savior.*** This is the only place in all the Gospels where Jesus is directly called Savior. This word is commonly used to describe God in the Old Testament as the one who rescues (Isa. 43:3,11; 49:6; Jer. 14:8) and so becomes yet another pointer to his deity.

SESSION 6
A HEALING AT BETHESDA

SCRIPTURE   JOHN 5:1–18

LAST WEEK

In last week's session we saw Jesus show great love and compassion for a woman of the hated Samaritan culture. As a result of that encounter, many people from the woman's town came to believe in Jesus as the "Savior of the world" (4:42). We were encouraged to step out of our own "comfort zone" and reach out to someone that we might feel an aversion for. This week we will look at Jesus' miraculous healing of an invalid at the pool of Bethesda, and consider what it says to us about our own need for healing.

ICE-BREAKER   15 Min.
CONNECT WITH YOUR GROUP

LEADER

Begin with a prayer that God will bless this time together. Choose one or two of the Ice-Breaker questions. If you have a new group member you may want to do all three.

We all need a little (or a lot!) of help at times from our family and friends. Sometimes we welcome that help and sometimes we resist. Jesus recognized that when he asked the invalid in today's story, "Do you want to get well?" Take turns sharing some of your experiences with needing help.

1. When you were injured as a child, how did you react?
    ❐ I didn't let anyone see me cry.
    ❐ I got help right away.
    ❐ I let all my emotions show.
    ❐ Other_____.

2. What is the longest that you remember being down with an illness or disability? Who was around to take care of you during this time? How do you remember feeling?

3. When you aren't able to change in the way you feel you ought to change, whom do you most frequently blame?

❏ Myself.

❏ My parents.

❏ God.

❏ Anyone else who happens to be around.

BIBLE STUDY   30 Min.

READ SCRIPTURE AND DISCUSS

LEADER

Select three members of the group ahead of time to read aloud the Scripture passage. Have one read John's narration; another read the part of Jesus; and another read the part of the invalid. Have the whole group read the part of the Jews in verses 10 and 12. Then have the group divide into subgroups of four or five to discuss the Questions for Interaction.

Jesus healed many people during his earthly ministry. Most frequently, however, he demanded that the person who wanted to be healed do something him or herself to show faith and thus take part in the healing. In the following story he has the disabled man take up his mat and walk. This is an important show of faith, and part of his healing, but it also raises some controversy between Jesus and certain hypercritical Pharisees. Read John 5:1–18 and note Jesus' response to the Jews who were persecuting him.

The Healing at the Pool

John:
> **5** *Some time later, Jesus went up to Jerusalem for a feast of the Jews. ²Now there is in Jerusalem near the Sheep Gate a pool, which in Aramaic is called Bethesda and which is surrounded by five covered colonnades. ³Here a great number of disabled people used to lie—the blind, the lame, the paralyzed. ⁵One who was there had been an invalid for thirty-eight years. ⁶When Jesus saw him lying there and learned that he had been in this condition for a long time, he asked him,*

Jesus: *"Do you want to get well?"*

Invalid: *⁷"Sir," the invalid replied, "I have no one to help me into the pool when the water is stirred. While I am trying to get in, someone else goes down ahead of me."*

Jesus: *⁸Then Jesus said to him, "Get up! Pick up your mat and walk."*

John: *⁹At once the man was cured; he picked up his mat and walked. The day on which this took place was a Sabbath, ¹⁰and so the Jews said to the man who had been healed,*

Jews:	*"It is the Sabbath; the law forbids you to carry your mat."*
Invalid:	*[11] But he replied, "The man who made me well said to me, 'Pick up your mat and walk.'"*
Jews:	*[12] So they asked him, "Who is this fellow who told you to pick it up and walk?"*
John:	*[13] The man who was healed had no idea who it was, for Jesus had slipped away into the crowd that was there. [14] Later Jesus found him at the temple and said to him,*
Jesus:	*"See, you are well again. Stop sinning or something worse may happen to you."*
John:	*[15] The man went away and told the Jews that it was Jesus who had made him well. [16] So, because Jesus was doing these things on the Sabbath, the Jews persecuted him. [17] Jesus said to them,*
Jesus:	*"My Father is always at his work to this very day, and I, too, am working."*
John:	*[18] For this reason the Jews tried all the harder to kill him; not only was he breaking the Sabbath, but he was even calling God his own Father, making himself equal with God.*

John 5:1–18

LEADER

Refer to the Summary and Study Notes at the end of this session as needed. If 30 minutes is not enough time to answer all of the questions in this section, conclude the Bible Study by answering questions #6 and #7.

QUESTIONS FOR INTERACTION

1. If you were in this man's condition and needed someone to help you get where you needed to be to find healing, who would you most likely rely on?

2. Why does Jesus ask this man whether or not he wants to get well? What might have been some reasons why he may *not* have wanted to get well?

3. What do you think of this man's reason for not being healed? Would you say that it is valid? Or is it simply a way of getting others to feel sorry for him?

4. Why do the Pharisees get upset with this man after Jesus heals him? What does their response say about their value system?

5. Why does Jesus say in verse 17, "My Father is always at his work to this very day"? Of what relevance is his statement to the questions raised about his healing someone on the Sabbath?

6. What fear or uncertainty seems to have you "paralyzed" at this point in your life? What would you say to Jesus were he to ask you, "Do you want to get well?"

7. What "first steps" do you need to take to be part of your own healing? What help could you use from others?

GOING DEEPER: *If your group has time and/or wants a challenge, go on to this question.*

8. The commandment that the Pharisees were trying to honor, "Remember the Sabbath day by keeping it holy," is actually scriptural (Ex. 20:8), yet their strict adherence to it brought them in conflict with Jesus, the Son of God. How can we tell when we also are holding to the letter of the law to the detriment of living according to the spirit of what God wants?

CARING TIME   15 Min.
APPLY THE LESSON AND PRAY FOR ONE ANOTHER

. . . .

LEADER

Be sure to save at least 15 minutes for this time of prayer and encouragement. Continue to encourage group members to invite new people to the group.

Help each other to the healing waters of Jesus' love during this time of sharing and prayer. After responding to the following questions, share prayer requests and close in a group prayer.

1. What season are you experiencing in your spiritual life right now?
  ❐ The warmth of summer.
  ❐ The dead of winter.
  ❐ The new life of spring.
  ❐ The changes of fall.

2. How has Jesus helped you "take up your mat and walk" in the past few weeks? What would you like to say to thank him?

3. How can this group support you in prayer with what you said you needed in questions #6 and #7? In what other ways can the group encourage you in your need?

NEXT WEEK

Today we discussed a healing Jesus did at the pool of Bethesda, and looked at it in relation to our own healing. We saw how Jesus asks us to participate in our healing and have faith that he will help us. In the coming week, pray that Jesus will use you to help others in the healing process. Next week we will study the incredible miracle of the feeding of the five thousand, and consider what it says about how God supplies all of our needs.

NOTES ON JOHN 5:1–18

Summary: Jesus healed many people. Generally they came to him asking to be healed, but this story is unusual because that apparently did not happen. In fact, Jesus had to ask the man if he wanted to be healed. Some people might think that the answer to such a question is obvious. Wouldn't a person who had suffered a disability for 38 years always want to be healed? But Jesus knew that sometimes a disability makes for a comfortable excuse—an excuse to feel sorry for one's self, an excuse to put the responsibility for one's well being on others. Sometimes a person doesn't want to let go of such excuses. That's why it was important that Jesus asked before healing this man. In the end, he decided that he wanted to be healed, and Jesus responded to his need.

However, this man's attitude wasn't the only obstacle Jesus had to face in this healing. There was also the legalistic attitude of the Pharisees. For them, the most important thing was not people, but the law. So what if a man who had been disabled for 38 years was healed? One must uphold the law!

The beauty of this story is the way it shows that Jesus is willing to step past all obstacles—those we put up ourselves and those put up by others—in order to help us find healing and wholeness. That is indeed worthy of being called "Good News"!

5:1 *feast of the Jews.* The three major Jewish festivals attracting pilgrims to Jerusalem were Passover, Pentecost and the Feast of Tabernacles. These specific feasts are mentioned elsewhere, but here there is no indication which one is in view.

5:2 *the Sheep Gate.* A gate in the east end of the north wall of Jerusalem, constructed when Nehemiah rebuilt that wall in 444 B.C. Since its location is near the temple, it may have been where sheep were brought in for the ritual sacrifices. *Bethesda.* The exact name is uncertain, but this pool has been excavated. Fed by intermittent springs, it was seen as a healing shrine even by second-century Roman cults.

5:7 *I have no one to help me.* The man had no prior expectation of Jesus as a healer. He was hopeful only that Jesus might assist him in getting into the water at the next available moment. ***when the water is stirred.*** This stirring of the water was probably caused by an intermittent spring, but was attributed to the action of a local divinity. The first people into the water after this stirring were the ones who were supposed to be healed.

5:8 ***Pick up your mat.*** The mat was a poor man's bed. Jesus gives this man something to do in order to take responsibility for his own life, his own healing. In the man's response in verse 7, he had essentially said it was out of his control—he had no one to help him. Jesus was bringing him healing, but he had to take some action on his own.

5:10 ***the law forbids you to carry your mat.*** This is an example of the traditions that the rabbis had developed over the years in an attempt to help people obey the Law.

5:13 ***had slipped away.*** Apparently Jesus had not identified himself in order to get credit for this healing.

5:14 ***Stop sinning or something worse may happen to you.*** Jesus did not accept the common idea that such infirmities as this man had suffered from were always the result of personal sin (9:1–3; see also Luke 13:1–5). However, it is sometimes true that sin has the natural consequence of physical illness. Constant worry can bring on ulcers. In some cases it has been found that unresolved guilt can even bring on paralysis. Perhaps this was true with this man, and Jesus saw it.

5:17 ***My Father is always at his work.*** The Sabbath is based on the idea that God rested on the seventh day. While Jesus does not dispute that one should honor the Sabbath, he points out that God is not now resting forever. His work of healing and redeeming continues, and Jesus, as the Son, is part of it.

Feeding the Five Thousand

Scripture John 6:1–15

LAST WEEK

Jesus' healing of the invalid at the pool of Bethesda was the focus of our study last week. We were reminded that Jesus knows our needs and will be there to help us, but he also wants us to participate in our own healing. This week we will take a look at the wondrous miracle of the feeding of the five thousand and be encouraged by what it says to us about God supplying our needs.

ICE-BREAKER   15 Min.
Connect With Your Group

LEADER

After beginning with a word of prayer, introduce and welcome new group members. If there are no new members, choose one or two of the Ice-Breaker questions to get started. If there are new members, then discuss all three.

Every day we are inundated with convenient and fast ways to meet our wants and needs. Our mail is full of credit card applications and TV commercials promise loans that will help us enjoy life to the fullest. In today's story, the disciples go to Jesus for help in meeting their needs. Take turns sharing how you have responded to times of need in your life.

1. When you were in grade school, did you most frequently bring your lunch, buy the school lunch or go home for lunch? Who did you like to eat lunch with? Did you share any of your lunch with him or her?

2. What kind of crowd are you most likely to be part of?
   ❏ A sports crowd.
   ❏ A concert crowd.
   ❏ A crowded shopping mall.
   ❏ A political rally.

   In that crowd, what are people most likely to not have enough of?

3. When in your life do you remember "a little going a long way"?

❏ When I was first married and tried to stretch a limited income.

❏ When I was in college and had to get by on limited sleep.

❏ When I was camping and forgot some supplies.

❏ Other _____.

How good are you at "making do?"

BIBLE STUDY

READ SCRIPTURE AND DISCUSS

30 Min.

LEADER

Ask a member of the group, selected ahead of time, to read aloud the Scripture passage. Then discuss the Questions for Interaction, dividing into subgroups of four or five.

Today, if you gather a crowd for any kind of event, you are most likely to have someone around setting up a concession stand. However, that was not the case in Jesus' day. When people came from miles around to hear him teach or to seek healing, they didn't always have access to enough food to eat. At least that was the case in the following story. Jesus' feeding of the five thousand was both an expression of his concern for the practical needs of people and his reassurance to us that, if we have faith in him, our needs will be supplied. Read John 6:1–15 and note the reaction of the crowd to Jesus' miracle.

Jesus Feeds the Five Thousand

6 Some time after this, Jesus crossed to the far shore of the Sea of Galilee (that is, the Sea of Tiberias), ²and a great crowd of people followed him because they saw the miraculous signs he had performed on the sick. ³Then Jesus went up on a mountainside and sat down with his disciples. ⁴The Jewish Passover Feast was near.

⁵When Jesus looked up and saw a great crowd coming toward him, he said to Philip, "Where shall we buy bread for these people to eat?" ⁶He asked this only to test him, for he already had in mind what he was going to do.

⁷Philip answered him, "Eight months' wages would not buy enough bread for each one to have a bite!"

⁸Another of his disciples, Andrew, Simon Peter's brother, spoke up, ⁹"Here is a boy with five small barley loaves and two small fish, but how far will they go among so many?"

¹⁰Jesus said, "Have the people sit down." There was plenty of grass in that place, and the men sat down, about five thousand of them. ¹¹Jesus then took the loaves, gave thanks, and distributed to those who were seated as much as they wanted. He did the same with the fish.

¹²When they had all had enough to eat, he said to his disciples, "Gather the pieces that are left over. Let nothing be wasted." ¹³So they gathered them and filled twelve baskets with the pieces of the five barley loaves left over by those who had eaten.

¹⁴After the people saw the miraculous sign that Jesus did, they began to say, "Surely this is the Prophet who is to come into the world." ¹⁵Jesus, knowing that they intended to come and make him king by force, withdrew again to a mountain by himself.

John 6:1–15

QUESTIONS FOR INTERACTION

LEADER

Refer to the Summary and Study Notes at the end of this session as needed. If 30 minutes is not enough time to answer all of the questions in this section, conclude the Bible Study by answering questions #6 and #7.

1. When do you remember being like the people in this crowd—away from home and caught with inadequate provisions? What did you do to remedy the situation?

2. What was the motivation of this crowd for following Jesus (v. 2)? Do you think they were looking for spiritual guidance or just personal benefit? Which one was your own motivation when you first came to Christ?

3. Why does Jesus ask Philip how they can feed all of the people, if he already knows how he is going to feed them? What might you have said if you were Philip in this situation?

4. How much provision did the boy provide and how much was left over? What point was Jesus trying to make by performing this miracle?

5. What causes Jesus to withdraw to a mountain by himself? What was he worried might happen, and why did that worry him?

6. When do you remember God providing for you when you were worried that you wouldn't have enough for your needs?

7. What big challenge are you facing in your life right now, where it seems that your resources for meeting the challenge are a paltry "five loaves and two small fish"?

GOING DEEPER: *If your group has time and/or wants a challenge, go on to this question.*

8. What should the balance be between a church ministering to physical needs like hunger and physical healing, and deeper, more spiritual needs? Should a ministry to physical needs be a "lure" to bring people to the spiritual, or should it be "no strings attached" caring?

CARING TIME   15 Min.
APPLY THE LESSON AND PRAY FOR ONE ANOTHER

LEADER

Continue to encourage group members to invite new people to the group. Remind everyone that this group is for learning and sharing, but also for reaching out to others. Close the group prayer by thanking God for each member and for this time together.

Take some time now to pray for one another, remembering that Jesus is there to abundantly meet your needs. Begin by sharing your responses to the following questions. Then share prayer requests and close with prayer.

1. Where do you see hungry or needy people in your community, and how can you pray that God will multiply the resources needed to feed them?

2. What would you especially like to thank God for in the way he responded to your need in the situation you spoke of in question #6?

3. Refresh your memories about the challenge faced by the person on your right (question #7). Pray that God will multiply his or her resources for this challenge.

NEXT WEEK

Today we considered the miracle of the feeding of the five thousand, and what it says about God supplying our needs. We were encouraged to go to Jesus with our needs, rather than depending on what the world offers. In the coming week, help someone in your church or neighborhood that you know is in need. Next week we will read about Jesus walking on water, and see the difference it makes for us when Christ is with us on our journey.

NOTES ON JOHN 6:1–15

Summary: The miracle of the feeding of the five thousand is quite frequently used as a story to talk about world hunger and the Christian response to it. That is an appropriate use of the story, since the story does show Christ's concern for the hungry, and since it shows how God can take what we offer and multiply it many times. However, this story is more than a hunger story. It is a story for any person who feels that his or her resources are inadequate to meet the challenges they face. And who has not faced such a situation? Sometimes it feels like we are looking through opposite ends of binoculars at the challenges ahead of us and the resources within us. We look at our challenges and they seem magnified, much larger than they often turn out to be. We look at our resources with those binoculars turned around, and they seem oh so tiny! God shows us that even if all we have is five loaves and two fish, it is enough when it is dedicated to God. God will multiply whatever we offer to him, and he will make it more than adequate to meet our challenge. But we must do two things: (1) we must offer what we have (What would have happened had the boy withheld his five loaves and two fish?), and (2) we must have faith in what God can do with what we offer him.

6:1 *the Sea of Tiberias.* Tiberias was a city founded on the shore of the Sea of Galilee in 20 A.D. by Herod. By the time this Gospel was written, this new name for the Sea of Galilee had become well known.

6:2 *the miraculous signs he had performed.* John uses the term "signs" to describe Jesus' miracles in order to encourage his readers not to see them simply as acts of power, but as pointers to God's presence in Jesus, seen by those who receive him (2:11,23; 3:2; 7:31; 9:16; 11:47; 12:37; 20:30). However, Jesus also warned that for many seeing signs was not enough (4:48; Matt. 12:38–39).

6:4 *The Jewish Passover Feast was near.* Passover celebrated Israel's deliverance from Egypt (Ex. 12:1–13). At that time, each family of Israel was to sacrifice a lamb, eat it and put its blood on the doorframe of their house so that God's avenging angel would "pass over" that house as Egypt was punished. Hence the lamb's blood was accepted in place of their first-

born, and its flesh nourished them for their escape from Egypt. Why does John mention the Passover at this point? Perhaps because Jesus reinterpreted Passover, relating it to his own sacrifice where his body was broken and his blood shed for many (Matt. 26:26–28), and the miracle he was about to do, the multiplying of bread and flesh (fish) for many was a symbolic type of that sacrifice.

6:9 *Here is a boy.* People will often say, "I am so small in the larger scheme of things; what could I possibly have to contribute?" This boy represents the answer to that question. One small boy contributing his small amount laid the groundwork for a great miracle of God! *five small barley loaves.* The poor used barley bread because it was less expensive than wheat. From Luke 11:5 we may assume that three loaves were normally a meal. At most the boy had provisions for two people. *how far will they go among so many?* The question asked by Andrew and Philip is similar to the response of

Moses when the people clamored for meat (Num. 11:21–23).

6:10 *about five thousand of them.* According to Matthew 14:21, this number did not include the women and children who were present. (Significantly, the boy who contributed the loaves and fish was probably among the unnumbered!)

6:14 *this is the Prophet.* The people see by this action that Jesus is far more than a healer, and that he has outdone anything accomplished by the prophets of old.

SESSION 8
JESUS WALKS ON WATER

SCRIPTURE   JOHN 6:16–27

LAST WEEK

We were encouraged last week by the miracle of the feeding of the five thousand and what it said to us about God supplying our needs. We saw how Jesus can multiply what we have and make it more than adequate to meet whatever challenge we're facing. This week we will consider Jesus' miracle of walking on water, and listen as he teaches the crowd, and us, to seek first the "food that endures to eternal life," instead of the "food that spoils" (v. 27).

ICE-BREAKER   15 Min.
CONNECT WITH YOUR GROUP

LEADER

Begin by praying for your group and your time together. Choose one, two or all three of the Ice-Breaker questions. Be sure to welcome and introduce new group members.

Fear and food are two of the topics that come up in today's Scripture passage. These are certainly things we can still relate to today! Share with the group some of your experiences and thoughts about fear and food.

1. When you were a child, what did you have a tendency to become afraid of when your parents weren't around?
   ❏ The dark.
   ❏ Noises in the house.
   ❏ The sound of the wind whipping around outside the house.
   ❏ Strangers at the door.
   ❏ Other_____.

   Where did you find reassurance?

2. What was your most memorable experience in a boat? What was your most frightening experience?

3. If a person wanted to motivate you with the promise of some kind of food, what kind of food should they use? What kind of food wouldn't work at all?

BIBLE STUDY   30 Min.
READ SCRIPTURE AND DISCUSS

LEADER

Ask a member of the group, selected ahead of time, to read aloud the Scripture passage. Then divide into subgroups of four or five and discuss the Questions for Interaction.

With his miracles of healing, Jesus showed himself to be Master over physical illness. With the miracle he does in the following story, he shows himself also to be Master over nature itself. His walking on water is one of the best-known signs of his divinity. It can also be seen as a promise that in him we can rise above the turmoil that is around us. Read John 6:16–27 and note how Jesus responds to the crowd.

Jesus Walks on Water

¹⁶When evening came, his disciples went down to the lake, ¹⁷where they got into a boat and set off across the lake for Capernaum. By now it was dark, and Jesus had not yet joined them. ¹⁸A strong wind was blowing and the waters grew rough. ¹⁹When they had rowed three or three and a half miles, they saw Jesus approaching the boat, walking on the water; and they were terrified. ²⁰But he said to them, "It is I; don't be afraid." ²¹Then they were willing to take him into the boat, and immediately the boat reached the shore where they were heading.

²²The next day the crowd that had stayed on the opposite shore of the lake realized that only one boat had been there, and that Jesus had not entered it with his disciples, but that they had gone away alone. ²³Then some boats from Tiberias landed near the place where the people had eaten the bread after the Lord had given thanks. ²⁴Once the crowd realized that neither Jesus nor his disciples were there, they got into the boats and went to Capernaum in search of Jesus.

²⁵When they found him on the other side of the lake, they asked him, "Rabbi, when did you get here?"

²⁶Jesus answered, "I tell you the truth, you are looking for me, not because you saw miraculous signs but because you ate the loaves and had your fill. ²⁷Do not work for food that spoils, but for food that endures to eternal life, which the Son of Man will give you. On him God the Father has placed his seal of approval."

John 6:16–27

QUESTIONS FOR INTERACTION

LEADER

Refer to the Summary and Study Notes at the end of this session as needed. If 30 minutes is not enough time to answer all of the questions in this section, conclude the Bible Study by answering questions #6 and #7.

1. Which part of this story do you identify with most strongly at this point in your life?
   ❒ Heading off on your own, leaving Jesus behind.
   ❒ Going through some "rough waters" and feeling afraid.
   ❒ Feeling the reassurance of Christ that you should not be afraid.
   ❒ Like the crowd, searching for Jesus.
   ❒ Seeking that which endures.
   ❒ Other_____.

2. Why do you think the disciples left Jesus behind and went out in the boat?
   ❒ They were leaving him because he wouldn't be king (v. 15).
   ❒ They were like his "roadies," going off to make advanced preparation for his next stop.
   ❒ He told them to because he wanted some time to himself.
   ❒ They didn't know where he was.
   ❒ Other_____.

3. Why were the disciples terrified (v. 19)?
   ❒ Because of the storm.
   ❒ Because Jesus appeared like a ghost, walking on water.
   ❒ Because they thought Jesus was angry with them for leaving him.
   ❒ Other_____.

4. Why do you think it took the crowd so long to discover that Jesus had left? If you had been part of the crowd, what "detective work" would you have done to find out where Jesus had gone?

5. What seems to be Jesus' attitude toward the crowd when they find him? What does he mean by the statement, "Do not work for food that spoils, but for food that endures to eternal life" (v. 27)?

6. When was there a period in your life when you went off on your own and left Jesus behind? Afterward, did you find him or did he find you?

7. At this point in your life, what are you looking for from Jesus? Is what you are looking for a physical, temporary benefit (like the bread and fish), or a long-term, spiritual benefit? What are you doing to "work for" this "food"?

GOING DEEPER: *If your group has time and/or wants a challenge, go on to this question.*

8. What kind of "work" can a person do to receive "food that endures to eternal life"? What are the relative roles of such work and the grace of God?

CARING TIME   15 Min.
APPLY THE LESSON AND PRAY FOR ONE ANOTHER

LEADER

Have you started working with your group about their mission—perhaps by sharing the dream of multiplying into two groups by the end of this study of John?

Encourage and support one another now with a time of prayer, remembering that since Jesus is with us on our journey we don't have to be afraid. He cares about every detail of our lives, both physical and spiritual. Take turns sharing your responses to these questions before closing in prayer.

1. What is your biggest concern about the coming week?

2. What is the nature of the "stormy waters" you have found yourself in most recently? How would you like Jesus to help you "rise above" these stormy waters?

3. Take time to thank God for those in your group who have found Jesus again after a period of leaving him behind.

NEXT WEEK

Today we read about Jesus walking on water, and how he calmed the fears of the disciples. We also listened as he taught his followers to be more concerned about their spiritual well being, rather than their earthly, physical needs. In the coming week, find a way to thank your pastor for helping you to stay focused on the "food that endures to eternal life." Next week we will discuss what it means that Jesus is the "bread of life," and how this belief leads us to everlasting life.

NOTES ON JOHN 6:16–27

Summary: Jesus often spent time alone in order to be spiritually renewed. He did this in the wilderness at the beginning of his ministry (Matt. 4:1–11), and at various other times during his ministry (Matt. 26:36–46; Mark 1:35–37). Just before this story, John tells us he "withdrew again to a mountain by himself" (6:15). It was while he was retreating in this way that the disciples left without him and headed off toward Capernaum. Why did they leave without Jesus? Perhaps they themselves didn't know where he had gone. Perhaps he had told them to go and make some preparations. (Matthew 14:22 indicates that this may have been the case.) We really can't tell from John's description. What we do know is that it set the scene for one of Jesus' greatest signs of who he was—walking on water. This was no ordinary rabbi! Nor was he just another magic man. The crowd had not yet grasped this. They looked to him as one who seemed able to provide for their needs, in some magical way. But they did not seem to understand as yet that this man was a special manifestation of God himself. In verses 26–27, Jesus seeks to redirect their thinking from looking for magical provision for physical need, to provision for the spiritual need that is at the heart of life.

6:19 *three or three and a half miles.* This would be about halfway across the lake. The lake, surrounded by hills, was often buffeted by strong winds sweeping across it. ***they were terrified.*** In Matthew's version we learn that the disciples thought they were seeing a ghost (Matt. 14:26).

6:20 *It is I.* While the disciples may have originally taken it only as a statement of identification, Jesus is saying that he is there, the Son of God who controls the wind and sea, so don't be afraid (Ps. 29:3; 77:19). ***don't be afraid.*** The call not to fear echoes God's assurance to Israel of his presence and protection. Isaiah 51:12, which was included in a reading normally done in the synagogues at Passover, focuses on the "I Am" who comforts his people. The story of the feeding and the walking on the water together validate Jesus' claims in John 5:19–23 since only God can perform these actions.

6:24 *Capernaum.* This was a town on the north end of the Sea of Galilee, three miles west of the Jordan River. It was a center of the fishing industry. Matthew 4:13 tells us that Jesus lived here and set it up as his base of operation, which would make it logical that when the people didn't find him, Capernaum would be where they would look.

6:25 *Rabbi, when did you get here?* Their real question of course is not "when," but "how"?

6:26 *not because you saw miraculous signs.* The crowd saw him only as a way to get their physical needs met.

6:27 *food that endures to eternal life.* Jesus challenges them to examine their priorities and to realize he has come to provide the "food" that will save people from spiritual hunger and death.

SESSION 9
THE BREAD OF LIFE

SCRIPTURE JOHN 6:28–51

LAST WEEK

In last week's session Jesus revealed his divine glory once again to his disciples by walking on the water and saving them from a dangerous storm. Jesus also reminded us that our priority in this life should be our spiritual well being, rather than our physical needs and worldly pursuits. This week we will look at what it means that Jesus is the Bread of Life, and how when we partake of this "bread that comes down from heaven" (v. 50), we will have everlasting life.

ICE-BREAKER   15 Min.
CONNECT WITH YOUR GROUP

LEADER

After beginning with a word of prayer, welcome and introduce new group members. Choose one, two or all three Ice-Breaker questions, depending on your group's needs.

"You are what you eat" is a mysterious phrase that we often hear. However, in the case of spiritual nourishment it takes on new meaning. Take turns sharing some of your unique life experiences with one another.

1. What kind of food is a traditional favorite in your family? Is there any food that goes way back in your ancestry, as something your family ate? Do you like this food yourself?

2. What is the hungriest you have ever been? What food finally relieved your hunger and where did you get it?

3. When was the last time you went back to the neighborhood where you were raised or one of the schools you attended? In what ways, if any, were people surprised about what you have done in your life?

BIBLE STUDY
READ SCRIPTURE AND DISCUSS

30 Min.

LEADER

As the group leader, read the part of Jesus in today's Scripture passage. Have the group members divide into two groups, with one group reading the part of "the questioning crowd" and the other group reading the part of "the grumblers." Then divide into smaller subgroups of four or five and discuss the Questions for Interaction.

The Gospel of John is not just about what Jesus did, but more importantly, who he was. This section helps define who he was as the Bread of Life, the one who came from heaven to give life to all who would believe.

Jesus the Bread of Life

Questioning Crowd: *²⁸Then they asked him, "What must we do to do the works God requires?"*

Jesus: *²⁹Jesus answered, "The work of God is this: to believe in the one he has sent."*

Questioning Crowd: *³⁰So they asked him, "What miraculous sign then will you give that we may see it and believe you? What will you do? ³¹Our forefathers ate the manna in the desert; as it is written: 'He gave them bread from heaven to eat.' "*

Jesus: *³²Jesus said to them, "I tell you the truth, it is not Moses who has given you the bread from heaven, but it is my Father who gives you the true bread from heaven. ³³For the bread of God is he who comes down from heaven and gives life to the world."*

Questioning Crowd: *³⁴"Sir," they said, "from now on give us this bread."*

Jesus: *³⁵Then Jesus declared, "I am the bread of life. He who comes to me will never go hungry, and he who believes in me will never be thirsty. ³⁶But as I told you, you have seen me and still you do not believe. ³⁷All that the Father gives me will come to me, and whoever comes to me I will never drive away. ³⁸For I have come down from heaven not to do my will but to do the will of him who sent me. ³⁹And this is the will of him who sent me, that I shall lose none of all that he has given me, but raise them up at the last day. ⁴⁰For my Father's will is that everyone who looks to the Son and believes in him shall have eternal life, and I will raise him up at the last day."*

The Grumblers: *⁴¹At this the Jews began to grumble about him because he said, "I am the bread that came down from heaven." ⁴²They said, "Is this not Jesus, the son of Joseph, whose father and mother we know? How can he now say, 'I came down from heaven'?"*

Jesus: *43"Stop grumbling among yourselves," Jesus answered. 44"No one can come to me unless the Father who sent me draws him, and I will raise him up at the last day. 45It is written in the Prophets: 'They will all be taught by God.' Everyone who listens to the Father and learns from him comes to me. 46No one has seen the Father except the one who is from God; only he has seen the Father. 47I tell you the truth, he who believes has everlasting life. 48I am the bread of life. 49Your forefathers ate the manna in the desert, yet they died. 50But here is the bread that comes down from heaven, which a man may eat and not die. 51I am the living bread that came down from heaven. If anyone eats of this bread, he will live forever. This bread is my flesh, which I will give for the life of the world."*

John 6:28–51

LEADER

Refer to the Summary and Study Notes at the end of this session as needed. If 30 minutes is not enough time to answer all of the questions in this section, conclude the Bible Study by answering questions #6 and #7.

QUESTIONS FOR INTERACTION

1. Had you been in Jesus' shoes (or, more appropriately, sandals!), how would you have reacted to the questions and responses of the crowd?
   ❑ Boy, are these guys thick.
   ❑ They really know how to ask the tough questions!
   ❑ I don't need this—I'm out of here!
   ❑ Other_____.

2. What does Jesus say "the work of God" is? What is the irony in describing that as a "work"?

3. Why does Jesus make a point of saying that it was God, not Moses, who gave the people the manna in the wilderness? How is Jesus a spiritual equivalent of that manna?

4. How many times in this passage does Jesus declare himself to be "the bread of life"? What does this phrase imply? How does he connect it later on to communion or the Lord's Supper?

5. What made those who grumbled especially cynical about Jesus' claim to be "the bread that came down from heaven" (vv. 41–42)?

6. How would you describe your own spiritual hunger right now?
   ❑ Starving.
   ❑ Ready for a "meal."
   ❑ Well-satisfied.
   ❑ Other_____.

7. If, as the saying goes, "Evangelism is one beggar telling another beggar where to find bread," what could you say to another beggar about where you have found "bread" in your life?

GOING DEEPER: *If your group has time and/or wants a challenge, go on to this question.*

8. Jesus says in verse 37, "All that the Father gives me will come to me." Is coming to Jesus a matter of God's choosing, our choosing or a combination of both?

CARING TIME 15 Min.
APPLY THE LESSON AND PRAY FOR ONE ANOTHER

LEADER

Have you identified someone in the group that could be a leader for a new small group when your group divides? How could you encourage and mentor that person?

For us to thrive as Christians we need more than study—we need support and encouragement. This is your time to give that to each other. Share your responses to the following questions before closing in prayer.

1. What do you look forward to the most about these meetings?

2. How can this group help you with the hunger you described in question #6? In what specific ways can the group pray for you?

3. Take time to thank God for those in your life who have helped you find "bread" when you were hungry.

NEXT WEEK

Today we discussed what it means that Jesus is the "bread of life." We were encouraged by the words of Jesus, "If anyone eats of this bread, he will live forever" (v. 51). In the coming week, think about how you can make the Lord's Supper more meaningful each time you participate. Next week we will consider those who questioned whether Jesus was the Christ, and we will see how Jesus and the Twelve respond to this desertion by many of those who were following him.

NOTES ON JOHN 6:28–51

Summary: In the Gospel of John, Jesus makes a series of "I am" statements. He says, "I am the light of the world"(8:12); "I am the gate for the sheep"(10:7); "I am the good shepherd"(10:11); "I am the way and the truth and the life"(14:6); and "I am the true vine"(15:1). Today's passage, where Jesus twice says, "I am the bread of life (vv. 35, 48), is the first in this series. This is, of course, a metaphor, and Jesus' hearers never seem to understand these metaphors. They can only think in terms of physical bread, like Moses gave their ancestors. When Jesus says that he also came from heaven, many are cynical because they know his father and mother and they think he was born to them in a normal way. They seem to think that coming from heaven precludes any sort of birth process. But Jesus essentially says to them that those who are sensitive to God and God's guidance will understand and follow him (vv. 44–51). It's no use for him to argue with those who do not have this sensitivity. The reward for those who do listen to God, and hence believe, is eternal life.

6:29 The crowd was looking for the law(s) Jesus wanted them to obey so they might have God's favor (v. 28). Jesus lets them see that only one thing is required (note the singular "work" in contrast to the plural "works"—v. 28): Belief in him is what is needed.

6:30 *What miraculous sign then will you give?* Some messianic expectations included the idea that the Messiah would display miracles greater than those of Moses. Since Jesus had only fed them once, they referred to this specific scene in hopes that he might provide for their needs in an ongoing way, as did Moses. *that we may see it and believe you.* The people were saying that if they saw miraculous signs, they would believe. However, they had already seen miraculous signs. Jesus warned that for many seeing signs was not enough (4:48; Matt. 12:38–39).

6:31 *Our forefathers ate the manna.* The story of the manna is told in Exodus, chapter 16.

6:34 *give us this bread.* This response is reminiscent of that of the Samaritan woman

when Jesus talked to her about living water (4:15). In both cases the hearer does not seem to fully comprehend what is being offered, but it sounds too good to pass up!

6:35 *I am the bread of life.* Just as bread is a basic food for the sustenance of physical life, so Jesus is a basic necessity for spiritual sustenance.

6:38 *For I have come down from heaven not to do my will.* The humility of Christ in coming to earth in obedience to the Father is also described in Philippians 2:1–11.

6:40 *my Father's will.* Two crucial themes, each stressing God's grace, are summed up here: (1) Salvation is open to all who believe Jesus, and (2) Salvation is a gift to be received. It is God's desire that all would accept his gift (2 Peter 3:9).

6:41 *the Jews.* This term is used in John in reference to the traditional Jewish leadership. Jesus and his disciples were, of course, Jews themselves.

6:42 *whose father and mother we know.* The Jews' point is that Jesus could not have come from heaven since he is a "local boy" and they remember when he was born. Their assumption, of course, was that Joseph was the biological father of Jesus, and that he was born in a normal way. This incident took place in Capernaum (v. 59), which was not far from Nazareth.

6:46 *No one has seen the Father except the one who is from God.* That no one has seen the Father is a point made several times by John. In John 1:18, he says that no one has seen the Father, but the Son makes him known. In 1 John 4:12, he says that no one has seen God, but if we love one another God lives in us. So the full picture that emerges from John is that even though no human has seen God, Jesus the Son of God has seen or experienced his nature directly, and has revealed his nature to his followers. These in turn, by imitating his love, reveal God's nature to others.

6:51 *for the life of the world.* Like the Passover lamb, his death means life to those who feed upon him.

IS JESUS THE CHRIST?

SCRIPTURE   JOHN 7:25–44

LAST WEEK

Last week we discussed what it meant that Jesus is the Bread of Life, and how all who come to him are never hungry or thirsty again. We were reminded of the great promise that "everyone who looks to the Son and believes in him shall have eternal life" (6:40). This week we will see how many doubted then, and many continue to doubt today, whether Jesus is indeed the Christ, the promised one of God.

ICE-BREAKER   15 Min.
CONNECT WITH YOUR GROUP

LEADER

Begin with a word of prayer and then discuss one, two or all three of the Ice-Breaker questions. Remember to stick closely to the three-part agenda and the time allowed for each segment.

Life is not without controversy, and many times we may find ourselves in the middle of misunderstandings or conflicts. Take turns sharing how you have handled times of controversy in your life.

1. Where do you consider yourself to be from? What are people from that country or region known for? Do you "fit the mold" of what people expect from those who are from this place?

2. In your family now, how often do you find that what you say is misunderstood? When was the last time people understood you to say something that was far different than you intended? What happened as a result?

3. Is there anything about you that sometimes causes people to get into an argument?

❏ My outspoken opinions.
❏ My offbeat sense of humor.
❏ My faith.
❏ Other_____.

If so, how do you feel about that?

BIBLE STUDY   30 Min.
READ SCRIPTURE AND DISCUSS

LEADER

Ask a member of the group, selected ahead of time, to read aloud the Scripture passage. Then discuss the Questions for Interaction, dividing into subgroups of four or five.

Once again, the Gospel of John focuses not just on what Jesus did, but on who he was. This passage concerns people who were wrestling with the most crucial question of all concerning who he was—was he indeed the Christ, the Promised One of God? Read John 7:25–44 and note the issues that made the people doubt who Jesus was.

Is Jesus the Christ?

²⁵At that point some of the people of Jerusalem began to ask, "Isn't this the man they are trying to kill? ²⁶Here he is, speaking publicly, and they are not saying a word to him. Have the authorities really concluded that he is the Christ? ²⁷But we know where this man is from; when the Christ comes, no one will know where he is from."

²⁸Then Jesus, still teaching in the temple courts, cried out, "Yes, you know me, and you know where I am from. I am not here on my own, but he who sent me is true. You do not know him, ²⁹but I know him because I am from him and he sent me."

³⁰At this they tried to seize him, but no one laid a hand on him, because his time had not yet come. ³¹Still, many in the crowd put their faith in him. They said, "When the Christ comes, will he do more miraculous signs than this man?"

³²The Pharisees heard the crowd whispering such things about him. Then the chief priests and the Pharisees sent temple guards to arrest him.

³³Jesus said, "I am with you for only a short time, and then I go to the one who sent me. ³⁴You will look for me, but you will not find me; and where I am, you cannot come."

³⁵The Jews said to one another, "Where does this man intend to go that we cannot find him? Will he go where our people live scattered among the Greeks, and teach the Greeks? ³⁶What did he mean when he said, 'You will look for me, but you will not find me,' and 'Where I am, you cannot come'?"

³⁷On the last and greatest day of the Feast, Jesus stood and said in a loud voice, "If anyone is thirsty, let him come to me and drink. ³⁸Whoever believes in me, as the Scripture has said, streams of living water will flow from within him." ³⁹By this he meant the Spirit, whom those who believed in him were later to receive. Up to that time the Spirit had not been given, since Jesus had not yet been glorified.

⁴⁰On hearing his words, some of the people said, "Surely this man is the Prophet."

⁴¹Others said, "He is the Christ."

Still others asked, "How can the Christ come from Galilee? ⁴²Does not the Scripture say that the Christ will come from David's family and from Bethlehem, the town where David lived?" ⁴³Thus the people were divided because of Jesus. ⁴⁴Some wanted to seize him, but no one laid a hand on him.

John 7:25–44

LEADER

Refer to the Summary and Study Notes at the end of this session as needed. If 30 minutes is not enough time to answer all of the questions in this section, conclude the Bible Study by answering question #7.

QUESTIONS FOR INTERACTION

1. These people were divided over who Jesus was. What causes people today to be divided over who Jesus is? Are the issues the same or different?

2. What seems to be the biggest objection the people have to the idea that Jesus might be the Christ? Why is that an issue to them?

3. When Jesus talks about where he is from (vv. 28–29), what does he mean? How is that different from what the people meant when they referred to where he was from?

4. What convinces those who put their faith in Jesus to make that decision? How does this compare to what convinced you to believe when you made your decision?

5. Why do the Pharisees want to arrest Jesus?
❏ Jealousy.
❏ Fear that he is leading the people astray.
❏ Fear that he might try to become king, and thus get Rome mad at them.
❏ Other_____.

6. To what is Jesus referring when he talks about "streams of living water" that will "flow from within" a person (v. 38)? Why is that an appropriate image?

7. How would you describe the "streams of living water" in your life right now?
❐ A roaring river.   ❐ A trickle.
❐ A quiet stream.   ❐ Other_____.

What might "increase the flow"?

GOING DEEPER: *If your group has time and/or wants a challenge, go on to this question.*

8. How is it that these people misunderstood virtually everything that Jesus said? What makes people more likely to understand spiritual truth?
❐ Intelligence.   ❐ Spiritual hunger.
❐ Open-mindedness.   ❐ Other_____.

CARING TIME   15 Min.
APPLY THE LESSON AND PRAY FOR ONE ANOTHER

LEADER

Conclude the group prayer today by reading 1 John 3:1–2: *How great is the love the Father has lavished on us, that we should be called children of God! And that is what we are! The reason the world does not know us is that it did not know him. Dear friends, now we are children of God, and what we will be has not yet been made known. But we know that when he appears, we shall be like him, for we shall see him as he is.*

Begin this Caring Time by sharing your responses to the following questions. Then take some time to share prayer requests and pray for one another.

1. The crowd asked many questions of Jesus in today's story. What question would you ask Jesus if he appeared to you today?

2. Who do you know who is as skeptical about Christ as the Pharisees in this story? How can the group pray for this person that he or she might open their heart?

3. Pray for the person on your right, that God might "increase the flow" of the Spirit in his or her life in the weeks to come.

NEXT WEEK

Today we looked at how people struggled with the question of whether Jesus was the Christ. We saw how they let many questions and doubts get in the way. In the coming week, continue to pray for the person you mentioned in question #2 under the Caring Time. Then spend some time with this person and ask the Holy Spirit to open his or her heart to who Jesus really is. Next week we will see the compassion of Jesus as he forgives the sins of the woman taken in adultery.

NOTES ON JOHN 7:25–44

Summary: Everyone who experienced the earthly ministry of Jesus knew he was a great teacher and a great healer. But Jewish history had seen many great teachers and even many healers. The real question that needed to be answered about Jesus was, "Is he truly the Christ, the unique Prophet sent from God to save his people?" That is the question the people wrestle with in this passage.

In deciding how they would answer this question there were two main issues: (1) Was Jesus' coming in line with what Scripture said concerning how he would come and where he would come from? and (2) Was he doing the kind of work the Scripture said that the Messiah would do? Those who rejected Jesus seemed to focus on the first question. According to their understanding, he didn't come from where he was supposed to come from. Scripture said that he should come from Bethlehem, and this man, so they thought, came from Nazareth. Perhaps they were not committed enough to find the truth and check out their assumptions about this. Those who put their faith in Jesus focused mostly on the second issue. They asked, "When the Christ comes, will he do more miraculous signs than this man?" (v. 31). Indeed no one before or since has done the kinds of things that Jesus did. But some people look right past such signs. For them it was true what Jesus said in another context: "If they do not listen to Moses and the Prophets, they will not be convinced even if someone rises from the dead" (Luke 16:31).

7:25 *trying to kill.* This desire to kill Jesus is mentioned in 5:18 and 7:1.

7:27 *But we know where this man is from.* They assumed that Jesus was from Nazareth in Galilee, and were most certainly not acquainted with the idea that he was born in Bethlehem. The Scriptures related the Messiah's origin to Bethlehem (Mic.

5:2), and later in this passage, this is pointed out (vv. 41–42). However, here the reference is to an expectation that the Messiah would appear "out of the blue" (based on an interpretation of Mal. 3:1). These people think since they were aware of Jesus' history, that this disqualifies him from being the Christ.

7:28–29 *you know where I am from ... I am from him.* Jesus turns around their phrase to establish that where he truly is from is from God.

7:30 *no one laid a hand on him.* While the authorities sought to seize him, Jesus was able to miraculously get away from them. Perhaps it was like the situation described in Luke 4:29–30, where we are told that when the people of the synagogue at Nazareth got angry at Jesus, "They got up, drove him out of the town, and took him to the brow of the hill on which the town was built, in order to throw him down the cliff. But he walked right through the crowd and went on his way." John says he was able to make such an escape because "his time had not yet come." This is to say that Jesus came to this world to die on a cross for the sins of the world, but the time for doing so had not yet come—he still had much to do in this life.

7:32 *chief priests and the Pharisees.* This is another way of referring to the Sanhedrin, the Jewish ruling Council.

7:34 *where I am, you cannot come.* When Jesus goes to his Father's side, his enemies will not be able to follow him.

7:35 *and teach the Greeks?* Just why they made this connection is unclear. Ironically, however, this mirrors exactly what the apostle Paul did. He left Jerusalem and went to the Jews dispersed among the Greeks. When these rejected the Gospel, he taught the Greeks (Gentiles) and led them to Christ.

7:37 *If anyone is thirsty, let him come to me and drink.* The vision in Ezekiel 47:1–12 of water flowing from the temple giving life to all the surrounding area is in view as Jesus, the new temple of God (2:19), provides the water of life to all who believe. This life is referring to the physical as well as spiritual.

7:39 *not yet been glorified.* This is another way of saying he had not yet died and been resurrected.

7:42 *from Bethlehem.* These people assumed that since Jesus was from Nazareth, he must have been born there. The story of Jesus' birth in Bethlehem was apparently not widely circulated.

SESSION 11
THE WOMAN CAUGHT IN ADULTERY

SCRIPTURE JOHN 8:2–11

LAST WEEK

Is Jesus the Christ? Last week we discussed the various reasons that the people debated and questioned if Jesus was truly the Messiah that they had been waiting for. Still others were convinced that this was the Christ because of his miraculous signs. This week we will look at another kind of debate—what to do with a woman who had been caught in the act of adultery. We will see how Jesus brings a new perspective and meaning to forgiveness.

ICE-BREAKER
CONNECT WITH YOUR GROUP
15 Min.

LEADER

Begin by praying for your group and your time together. Choose one, two or all three Ice-Breaker questions, depending on your group's needs.

A popular saying found on t-shirts today is, "I didn't do it!" We've probably all been in situations where we did something wrong and then denied it. Take turns sharing some of your experiences with right and wrong.

1. When do you remember being caught "red-handed" doing something as a child or adolescent that you weren't supposed to do? How did your parents handle the situation?

2. When you got into trouble as a child, who was most likely to take your defense? Who was most likely to "take the stand" against you?

3. When were you last asked to stand in judgment on someone?
- ❒ In a jury.
- ❒ On a search or personnel committee.
- ❒ When two of your kids blamed something on each other.
- ❒ Other_____.

How did it feel being in this position?

BIBLE STUDY   30 Min.
READ SCRIPTURE AND DISCUSS

. . . .

LEADER

Select five members of the group ahead of time to read aloud the Scripture passage. Have one group member read the part of John, the narrator; one person the part of Jesus; one person the part of the woman; and two people the part of the Pharisees. Then discuss the Questions for Interaction, dividing into subgroups of four or five.

The following story, whose status in the earliest manuscripts of John is uncertain, is nevertheless one of the best-known and most-loved stories of God's forgiveness. Through this story we are clearly called to show the kind of forgiveness to others that we want God to show to us.

John: *²At dawn he [Jesus] appeared again in the temple courts, where all the people gathered around him, and he sat down to teach them. ³The teachers of the law and the Pharisees brought in a woman caught in adultery. They made her stand before the group ⁴and said to Jesus,*

Pharisees: *"Teacher, this woman was caught in the act of adultery. ⁵In the Law Moses commanded us to stone such women. Now what do you say?"*

John: *⁶They were using this question as a trap, in order to have a basis for accusing him. But Jesus bent down and started writing on the ground with his finger. ⁷When they kept on questioning him, he straightened up and said to them,*

Jesus: *"If any one of you is without sin, let him be the first to throw a stone at her."*

John: *⁸Again he stooped down and wrote on the ground. ⁹At this, those who heard began to go away one at a time, the older ones first, until only Jesus was left, with the woman still standing there. ¹⁰Jesus straightened up and asked her,*

Jesus: *"Woman, where are they? Has no one condemned you?"*

Woman:	[11] *"No one, sir," she said.*
Jesus:	*"Then neither do I condemn you," Jesus declared. "Go now and leave your life of sin."*

John 8:2–11

LEADER

Refer to the Summary and Study Notes at the end of this session as needed. If 30 minutes is not enough time to answer all of the questions in this section, conclude the Bible Study by answering question #7.

QUESTIONS FOR INTERACTION

1. What shocks you the most about this story?
❐ That the man wasn't hauled before Jesus as well.
❐ That they really would consider executing a woman for such an act.
❐ That religious people would use this woman as a pawn to get at Jesus.
❐ That the accusers could be silenced so easily.
❐ Other _____.

2. What is the trap the Pharisees are setting for Jesus? What would it have done to his credibility as a teacher if he would have spoken against what was in the Law of Moses? What would it have done to his status as a compassionate teacher of the people if he had called for her to be stoned?

3. What do you think Jesus was writing on the ground with his finger (see note on 8:6)? Why does he not answer them at first?

4. Who does Jesus call upon to cast the first stone at this woman? Why does he establish this as the criteria?

5. Why do you think that the older Pharisees left first? What does this say about the experience of getting older?

6. When do you remember last receiving a merciful response to something you had done wrong? How did this mercy affect your resolve to not repeat the act?

7. Had Jesus said to you, "Then neither do I condemn you. Go now and leave your life of sin," how would you have responded?

❏ "Easier said than done."

❏ "I'll try."

❏ Simply, "Thank you, Lord."

❏ Other_____.

What help would you need to follow this directive?

GOING DEEPER: *If your group has time and/or wants a challenge, go on to this question.*

8. What does this story say about the idea that what is needed today to discourage wrong behavior is stricter laws and more stringent punishments? What are the relative roles of punishment and mercy in changing people's behavior?

CARING TIME   15 Min.
APPLY THE LESSON AND PRAY FOR ONE ANOTHER

LEADER

Conclude the prayer time today by asking God for guidance in determining the future mission and outreach of this group.

Take time to pray for one another and support one another, remembering the forgiveness that Jesus shows to each of us. Respond to the following questions before closing in prayer.

1. Make a list of the people who have been merciful to you in your life (responses to question #6 will give you a good start). Take time to thank God for these people.

2. Who do you know who is morally struggling, and could use the prayers of this group?

3. If you were in a group to whom Jesus said, "If any of you is without sin, let him be the first to cast a stone," what sin of your own would come to mind? Take time to pray for forgiveness for these sins and strength to deal with them in the future.

Today we looked at the well-known example of Jesus forgiving the sins of the woman caught in adultery. We were comforted by the compassion and mercy of Jesus. In the coming week, make a list of sins you've been struggling with, ask Jesus for forgiveness and then destroy the list, knowing that those sins are not only forgiven, but forgotten. Next week we will consider how sins like this woman's can enslave a person, even those who consider themselves to be religious. We will also see what it means to be truly a child of God.

NOTES ON JOHN 8:2–11

Summary: Jesus was not one who only helped people find physical healing. More importantly, he helped people find spiritual healing through forgiveness. That is what the people of that time needed most of all. The Pharisees only provided oppressive laws that weighed them down. In the case of this week's story, these laws even threatened to take away life. The Law of Moses had called upon those who committed adultery to be stoned. This penalty was rarely carried out, but it was there nonetheless. The woman brought before Jesus was apparently guilty of this sin—caught in the very act.

Would the Pharisees have executed her had Jesus given them the go-ahead? We don't know. What we do know is the words that Jesus said to save her, words that have been said many times since to discourage judgmental behavior—"Let the one who is without sin be the first to cast a stone." As he was setting her free he made one more important pronouncement—"Go now and leave your life of sin." God's forgiveness is always meant to lead us to repentance and a moral turn-around. Did this woman end up making such a change in her life? Again, we don't know for sure. But we do know that the forgiveness of God through Jesus Christ has turned many lives like hers around, and it was probably true of her as well. That is the nature of the hope that Christ brings.

8:3 *teachers of the law and the Pharisees.* They were the ordained teachers, serving as the representatives of Moses to the people in interpreting the Law. They were taught as rabbis and acted as lawyers in legal cases. ***a woman caught in adultery.*** Since this sin cannot be committed alone, why was only one offender brought before the temple courts? The teachers of the Law and the Pharisees had staged this to trap Jesus (v. 6), and provision had been made for the man to escape.

8:5 *Moses commanded us to stone such women.* This was only partially true. Leviticus 20:10 and Deuteronomy 22:22 prescribe that both parties shall be put to death. Since it was said that the woman was caught in the act, the man was also there and should have been brought in as well. The Jews, under Roman law, had no authority to carry out such sentences. In Israel's past, this penalty was rarely carried out because capital offenses required two or three witnesses. The normal result of adultery (on the part of a woman) was divorce. Women could not divorce their husbands for any reason.

8:6 *They were using this question as a trap.* See also Matthew 19:3 and 22:15 for other situations where Jesus' enemies attempted to get some reason for making a charge against him. In this case, if he allowed stoning he would be in violation of Roman law and would be found to be stricter than even the Pharisees in his application of the Law. If he tried to release her, he could be faulted for ignoring the Law of Moses. ***started to write on the ground with his finger.*** It is uncertain what Jesus wrote. However, speculation centers on the possibility that he was writing the other commandments, which would remind onlookers of commandments *they* may have broken. Significantly, the commandments of the Law were said to have been written on the stone tablets by the finger of God (Ex. 31:18).

8:7 *If any one of you is without sin.* Jesus affirms the validity of the Law, but forces the initiative back on the accusers. Perhaps some of them had in the back of their memory a time when they "sowed some wild oats." This statement does not imply that only sinless people can try judicial cases. It is, however, a rebuke to the base motives of these leaders who would self-righteously forget their own sins while using this woman to implicate Jesus.

8:9 *the older ones first.* The older ones may have had the wisdom of experience to know their own fallibilities. The younger ones may not have been old enough to have their eyes fully open to see themselves as they were.

8:11 *neither do I condemn you.* This story illustrates the truth of John 3:17. The woman had come face-to-face with condemnation, shame and death, but was pardoned by the one to whom all judgment has been given (5:22). ***Go now and leave your life of sin.*** The compassion and mercy of Jesus is related to his call to people to live in obedience to the will of his Father. Paul, likewise, flatly rejects the idea that people can claim God's mercy while actively pursuing a lifestyle that is in opposition to his will (Rom. 6:1–2,15).

SESSION 12
THE CHILDREN OF ABRAHAM

SCRIPTURE JOHN 8:31–47

LAST WEEK

We were reminded last week of the beautiful compassion and mercy of Jesus as we considered the way he treated a woman who had been caught in the act of adultery. We also discussed how the forgiveness of God through Jesus Christ is meant to lead us to repentance and a turning away from our lives of sin. This week we will listen in on a conversation Jesus has with some of the religious authorities and see how he tries to convince them of a hard truth—that if they don't believe in him they are actually children of the devil rather than children of Abraham.

ICE-BREAKER
CONNECT WITH YOUR GROUP

15 Min.

LEADER

Begin with a prayer that God will bless this time together. Choose one, two or all three of the Ice-Breaker questions, depending on your group's needs.

Our ancestry and heritage is often a large part of our identity and we feel a special link with other family and friends who share that. Take turns sharing your experiences with important people in your life.

1. What physical characteristics and mannerisms did you inherit from your father? What personality traits do you have that are like him?

2. What predecessor in your line of work or profession do you consider yourself to be a "child" of?—someone whose philosophies or approach you have admired or emulated?

3. With whom do you most frequently have a "language difficulty," where you don't seem to be getting through to each other?

☐ My spouse.

☐ My teenage children.

☐ People at work from a different culture.

☐ Other_____.

BIBLE STUDY

READ SCRIPTURE AND DISCUSS

30 Min.

LEADER

Ask a member of the group, selected ahead of time, to read aloud the Scripture passage. Then discuss the Questions for Interaction, dividing into subgroups of four or five.

Many of the Jewish religious leaders of Jesus' time based their status before God on the fact that they were children of Abraham, through whom the promise was given. But in the following story Jesus tells them that they are really children of the devil, and need to be freed from his power. Through this story we also are warned that our status before God is not based on parentage, but on hearing and obeying the call of God. Read John 8:31–47 and note how Jesus emphasizes the contrast between truth and lies.

The Children of Abraham

³¹To the Jews who had believed him, Jesus said, "If you hold to my teaching, you are really my disciples. ³²Then you will know the truth, and the truth will set you free."

³³They answered him, "We are Abraham's descendants and have never been slaves of anyone. How can you say that we shall be set free?"

³⁴Jesus replied, "I tell you the truth, everyone who sins is a slave to sin. ³⁵Now a slave has no permanent place in the family, but a son belongs to it forever. ³⁶So if the Son sets you free, you will be free indeed. ³⁷I know you are Abraham's descendants. Yet you are ready to kill me, because you have no room for my word. ³⁸I am telling you what I have seen in the Father's presence, and you do what you have heard from your father."

³⁹"Abraham is our father," they answered.

"If you were Abraham's children," said Jesus, "then you would do the things Abraham did. ⁴⁰As it is, you are determined to kill me, a man who has told you the truth that I heard from God. Abraham did not do such things. ⁴¹You are doing the things your own father does."

"We are not illegitimate children," they protested. "The only Father we have is God himself."

42Jesus said to them, "If God were your Father, you would love me, for I came from God and now am here. I have not come on my own; but he sent me. 43Why is my language not clear to you? Because you are unable to hear what I say. 44You belong to your father, the devil, and you want to carry out your father's desire. He was a murderer from the beginning, not holding to the truth, for there is no truth in him. When he lies, he speaks his native language, for he is a liar and the father of lies. 45Yet because I tell the truth, you do not believe me! 46Can any of you prove me guilty of sin? If I am telling the truth, why don't you believe me? 47He who belongs to God hears what God says. The reason you do not hear is that you do not belong to God."

John 8:31–47

QUESTIONS FOR INTERACTION

LEADER

Refer to the Summary and Study Notes at the end of this session as needed. If 30 minutes is not enough time to answer all of the questions in this section, conclude the Bible Study by answering question #7.

1. How would you have reacted had Jesus said to you, "You will know the truth and the truth will set you free"?
   ❐ Like his listeners, "I'm free already!"
   ❐ Like in the movie, *A Few Good Men*, "I can't handle the truth!"
   ❐ Like a '60s protester, "Freedom now!"
   ❐ Simply, "I'm ready, Lord."
   ❐ Other_____.

2. How do Jesus' listeners misunderstand what he is offering? How is their concept of "freedom" different from his?

3. When people are apart from the Son, to what are they enslaved? How does Jesus free them from this?

4. Based on what he says in this chapter, what do you think Jesus would say it means to be "free indeed"? What does this say about the emphasis in our own country on various "freedoms"?

5. What explanation does Jesus give for the fact that these people kept misunderstanding what he said? How does his explanation relate to who he said their father was?

6. How free do you feel you are at this point in your life?
- ❏ As free as a bird.
- ❏ As free as a bird with limited flight ability.
- ❏ More like a caged bird.
- ❏ Other_____.

7. What needs to happen in order for you to be "free indeed"? What enslaving sin do you need to let go of? What word do you need to hear from Jesus?

GOING DEEPER: *If your group has time and/or wants a challenge, go on to this question.*

8. What does this encounter say about why people may not respond to our witness? Should this be an excuse to give up and dismiss them easily? What implications are there for how we go about witnessing?

CARING TIME   15 Min.
APPLY THE LESSON AND PRAY FOR ONE ANOTHER

. . . .

LEADER

Following the Caring Time, discuss with your group how they would like to celebrate the last session next week. Also, discuss the possibility of splitting into two groups and continuing with another study.

Remembering that God is our Father, go to him now in a time of sharing and prayer. After responding to the following questions, share prayer requests and close in a group prayer.

1. What was the low point of your week last week? What was the high point?

2. Who do you know who is rejecting Christ at this moment of their life? Pray that God will help them hear His call.

3. Take time to pray that the person to your right be free indeed by overcoming the enslavement he or she talked about in question #7.

Today we saw Jesus clearly explain what it means to truly be a child of God. We were warned about getting caught up in lies and sin and how that can enslave us. On the other hand, we were promised that we can be free indeed if we put our faith in Jesus and follow him. In the coming week, remember to thank God daily for the freedom He has brought to your life. Next week we will look at Christ's role as the Good Shepherd who not only leads his sheep, but also lays down his life for them.

NOTES ON JOHN 8:31–47

Summary: The United States prides itself on freedom, freedom our ancestors fought for. In one sense we should be proud of this since our nation has fought hard for it, and since our democratic freedom has led the way for other nations to also obtain these freedoms. However, in another sense our nation has not done a good job in defining what freedom really means and how our freedoms should be used. Is a drug addict lying in a gutter truly free because that gutter is in America? Jesus pointed out that the most enslaving influences of life could be our own addictions and compulsions, our own *sin*. That was true for the Jews of Jesus time, and it is true for us today. Just as these Jewish people thought they were automatically free by virtue of their lineage, we think we are automatically free by virtue of our American citizenship. But our nation, which has taken the lead in procuring freedom, would do well to follow the one who took the lead in defining it. "So if the Son sets you free, you will be free indeed" (v. 36).

8:31 *the Jews who had believed in him.* These are the ones referred to in verse 39. Their later doubt shows that they are like those in the parable of the sower, where the seed fell on shallow soil and sprang up quickly, but later withered because it had no root (Matt. 13:5–6).

8:32 the truth will set you free. The truth being referred to here is that which comes through Christ, not some vague philosophical notion of truth. Jesus later says, "I am the way and the truth and the life" (14:6).

8:34 *everyone who sins is a slave to sin.* Paul expands on this point in Romans 6:15–23. We can see this most clearly in addictions like alcohol and drug abuse, but it is no less true in sins like greed and materialism, where our possessions often end up "owning us."

8:36 *if the Son sets you free.* The source of spiritual freedom is found in Jesus. This kind of freedom is more than political freedom, where we are free to do what our desires direct. Those desires frequently lead us into compulsive behaviors that destroy us and take away our true freedom. To be free indeed means to be free to realize our fullest potential; to be what God created us to be.

8:37 *ready to kill me.* See also 5:18, 7:1 and 7:25.

8:39 *If you were Abraham's children.* Paul argues that the true children of Abraham are not the physical descendants, but those who believe the promise of God (Rom. 9:6–8). Jesus says in Matthew 3:9 that God could raise up children of Abraham out of the stones around him.

8:41 *your own father.* Having denied that they are Abraham's children in verse 40,

Jesus' statement here raises the question of whose children they really are. Jesus claims they are really children of the devil (v. 44). ***We are not illegitimate.*** The irregular circumstances behind Jesus' birth are probably in view in this passage. Although Mary became pregnant before her marriage through the Holy Spirit, in the eyes of the people, they probably saw it as an illegitimate birth.

8:44 *a murderer from the beginning.* Satan was identified with the serpent that deceived Eve and brought sin into the world, which eventually led to the murder of Abel by Cain. 1 John 3:8 says, "He who does what is sinful is of the devil, because the devil has been sinning from the beginning."

THE GOOD SHEPHERD

SCRIPTURE   JOHN 10:1–21

LAST WEEK

In last week's session we discussed what it means to be truly free, and how through Christ we can have that freedom. We were encouraged by the fact that we are now part of God's family and he is our Father. This week we will look at Jesus' claim to be the Good Shepherd, and how he watches after us and leads us. We will also consider his promise, "I have come that they may have life, and have it to the full" (v. 10).

ICE-BREAKER   15 Min.
CONNECT WITH YOUR GROUP

LEADER

Begin this final session with a word of prayer and thanksgiving for this time together. Choose one or two Ice-Breaker questions to discuss.

The image of Jesus as the Good Shepherd in today's passage is a beautiful reminder of how much God cares for us, loves us and protects us. Take turns sharing more of your unique life experiences as you begin this last session together.

1.   What animal or animals did you help take care of as a child growing up? What did you do to help care for them?

2.   When you were a child or adolescent, when did you go somewhere and not enter by the gate?
❏ When I sneaked into a movie, ballgame or circus.
❏ When I sneaked out of the house.
❏ When I crashed a party.
❏ Other_____.

Did you get discovered?

3. When you were in high school, who were the "wolves" that most threatened your "pen," your sense of safety and security?

❑ Gangs.
❑ Hostile teachers.
❑ Druggies.
❑ Other_____.

BIBLE STUDY   30 Min.
Read Scripture and Discuss

Jesus lived in a pastoral culture where shepherding and fishing were the primary industries. Thus the images he most frequently used related to this culture. In the following passage, he refers to himself as both "the good shepherd" and the "gate" of the sheep. With these images he reassured the people of that time—and us—of his watchful care. Read John 10:1–21 and note the reaction of the Jews he was talking with.

The Shepherd and His Flock

10 *"I tell you the truth, the man who does not enter the sheep pen by the gate, but climbs in by some other way, is a thief and a robber. ²The man who enters by the gate is the shepherd of his sheep. ³The watchman opens the gate for him, and the sheep listen to his voice. He calls his own sheep by name and leads them out. ⁴When he has brought out all his own, he goes on ahead of them, and his sheep follow him because they know his voice. ⁵But they will never follow a stranger; in fact, they will run away from him because they do not recognize a stranger's voice." ⁶Jesus used this figure of speech, but they did not understand what he was telling them.*

⁷Therefore Jesus said again, "I tell you the truth, I am the gate for the sheep. ⁸All who ever came before me were thieves and robbers, but the sheep did not listen to them. ⁹I am the gate; whoever enters through me will be saved. He will come in and go out, and find pasture. ¹⁰The thief comes only to steal and kill and destroy; I have come that they may have life, and have it to the full.

¹¹"I am the good shepherd. The good shepherd lays down his life for the sheep. ¹²The hired hand is not the shepherd who owns the sheep. So when he sees the wolf coming, he abandons the sheep and runs away. Then the wolf attacks the flock and scatters it. ¹³The man runs away because he is a hired hand and cares nothing for the sheep.

[14]"I am the good shepherd; I know my sheep and my sheep know me—[15]just as the Father knows me and I know the Father— and I lay down my life for the sheep. [16]I have other sheep that are not of this sheep pen. I must bring them also. They too will listen to my voice, and there shall be one flock and one shepherd. [17]The reason my Father loves me is that I lay down my life—only to take it up again. [18]No one takes it from me, but I lay it down of my own accord. I have authority to lay it down and authority to take it up again. This command I received from my Father."

[19]At these words the Jews were again divided. [20]Many of them said, "He is demon-possessed and raving mad. Why listen to him?"

[21]But others said, "These are not the sayings of a man possessed by a demon. Can a demon open the eyes of the blind?"

John 10:1–21

LEADER

Refer to the Summary and Study Notes at the end of this session as needed. If 30 minutes is not enough time to answer all of the questions in this section, conclude the Bible Study by answering question #7.

QUESTIONS FOR INTERACTION

1. When in your life have you found yourself "following a stranger"—a person who eventually led you astray?

2. Who does Jesus call "thieves and robbers" (v. 8)? Why do they deserve this designation?

3. What are the various things listed or implied in this chapter that the Good Shepherd does for the sheep? Which of these things are most important to you right now?

4. Who might have been the "wolves" of the time from whom Jesus, the Good Shepherd, needed to protect the people?

5. Who are the "other sheep" that Jesus is talking about in verse 16? Why does he feel it to be important that he tell about these other sheep?

6. Which of the images of this chapter best describes your life right now?
   ❏ Feeling secure in my "pen."
   ❏ Feeling abandoned by the one who was supposed to watch over me.
   ❏ Not knowing whom to follow because all I hear is the voice of strangers.
   ❏ Hearing and following Jesus' voice.
   ❏ Other_____.

7. What "wolf" is most threatening your life right now? How can the Good Shepherd help you find protection from this "wolf"?

GOING DEEPER: *If your group has time and/or wants a challenge, go on to this question.*

8. What does it mean to have life "to the full" (v. 10)? Do Christians really have fuller lives than non-Christians? Why or why not?

CARING TIME   15 Min.
APPLY THE LESSON AND PRAY FOR ONE ANOTHER

. . . .

LEADER

Conclude this final Caring Time by praying for each group member and asking for God's blessing in any plans to start a new group and/or continue to study together.

Gather around each other now in this final time of sharing and prayer and encourage one another to have faith as you go back out into the world, remembering that "He [Jesus] calls his own sheep by name and leads them out" (v. 3).

1. How do you need Jesus to "shepherd" you at this time in your life?

2. How has this group been a "safe pen" for you during the time we have met? What have you especially appreciated about what you have received in this group?

3. What are you most missing to have life "to the full"? How can the members of this group continue to pray for you so that you may have life "to the full"?

WHAT'S NEXT?

Today we were reassured and comforted by Jesus, as he compared himself to a good shepherd, always looking after the welfare of his flock. Jesus loves us so much that, as the Good Shepherd, he laid down his life to save us from sin and death. If your group has decided to study Book 2 of John, you will continue to see a beautiful portrait painted of Jesus and a unique perspective on his life.

NOTES ON JOHN 10:1–21

Summary: In a country where the population is largely urban and suburban, and where even the farms are often run by large conglomerates, it is ironic that one of the most popular Scriptures starts, "The Lord is my shepherd, I shall not be in want" (Ps. 23:1). While our culture does not really understand all the ins and outs of shepherding, we do seem to sense that it has to do with looking out after the vulnerable, and we hunger for that kind of watchful care over us. That is why it still strikes home to us when Jesus says in this chapter that he is the Good Shepherd. He is the one who will protect us from the "wolves" of our society—the drug dealers, the users and abusers of life. He is also the one who will protect us from ourselves when, like sheep, we wander off into dangerous areas, from which we cannot find our own way back. Others may claim this kind of protection and caring, but it is most often with a price. They are the "hired hands" Jesus talks about (v. 12). But Jesus' love and concern for us is so deep that he gave his life for us. That truly is the kind of good shepherd so many of us long for.

10:1 *sheep pen.* Sheep were herded into stonewall enclosures at night as a protection against predators and thieves.

10:3 *The watchman.* Although both the shepherd and the gate clearly represent Jesus (vv. 7, 11), the figure of the watchman is not explained. In a parable, unlike an allegory, not all details have a meaning. ***calls his own sheep by name.*** Shepherds had names and calls for their sheep as a means of aiding them in separating their flocks from mixed herds such as would be found in a typical sheep pen.

10:7 *I am the gate.* This symbol is stated forthrightly in 14:6, where Jesus says he is the way to God.

10:8 *thieves and robbers.* In this context, Jesus is referring to the religious leaders who exploit the people for their own ends (2:14–16; Ezek. 34:1–6).

10:10 *have it to the full.* The eternal life one has in Christ has to do with more than length of life, but quality of life as well.

10:11 *I am the good shepherd.* In contrast to the hired hands who run away at danger, the true shepherd cares for the flock at his own risk (1 Sam. 17:34–35). The image of the ruler as a shepherd was a very common one in Israel (Ps. 23; Ezek. 34).

10:14 *I know my sheep.* "To know" is equivalent with "to love" (v. 15).

10:15 *I lay down my life.* This phrase accents the voluntary nature of his death (v. 18).

10:16 *I have other sheep that are not of this sheep pen.* Since this Gospel has consistently stressed that Jesus' mission was not just to Jews but to all the world, it is likely that this is the meaning here also. The "other sheep" would be Gentile believers. ***one flock and one shepherd.*** The Christian community is not to be marred by divisions, but is to model unity across racial and ethnic lines as all respond to the voice of the one shepherd (11:52; Eph. 2:11–22).

Other great resources
from Serendipity House...

MORE

More depth, more meaning, more life.

Discovering truth through Bible study is much more than breaking a verse down to its smallest part and deconstructing a passage word by word. There is context and experience, mystery and story that all go into fully understanding the Word of God. By dissecting down to the smallest part, we often lose the essence of the whole. For this reason, Serendipity introduces a new approach to the inductive Bible-study format that looks at each passage within the context of the larger story. This reunifies the cognitive aspect with an experiential dynamic and allows the truths of scripture to come alive in new and unexpected ways.

Song of Songs: The Epic Romance | 1574943405
Job: A Messy Faith | 1574943464

Mark: Beyond the Red Letters | 1574943413
Colossians: Embrace the Mystery | 1574944150

GOD AND THE ARTS

Where faith intersects life.

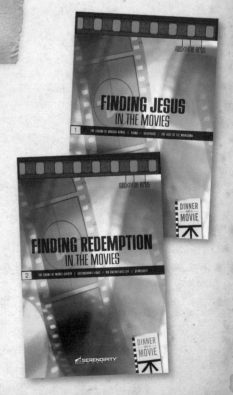

Stories, great and small, share the same essential structure because every story we tell borrows its power from a Larger Story. What we sense stirring within is a heart that is made for a place in the Larger Story. It is no accident that great movies include a hero, a villain, a betrayal, a battle to fight, a romance, and a beauty to rescue. It is The Epic story and it is truer than anything we know. Adventure awaits. Listen.

Discover an experience that guides you on a journey into the one great Epic in which the Bible is set. These fun and provocative studies features four films, each with two small-group meetings, *Dinner and a Movie* (Week 1), *Connecting the Dots* (Week 2), and an *Experience Guide* that offers valuable insights.

Finding Jesus in the Movies | 1574943553
Finding Redemption in the Movies | 1574943421

Personal Notes

Personal Notes